LORD NELSON

MAKERS OF HISTORY

MAKERS OF HISTORY

LORD NELSON

by

CAROLA OMAN *Lenanton*

ARCHON BOOKS
Hamden, Connecticut

First Published in 1954
First Published in the 'Makers of History' Series 1968
First Published in the United States of America 1968

Contents

Plates

Maps

* 1 *

"Nephew to Captain Suckling"

ON AN early spring day of 1776, a midshipman
who was not expected to live, a dreadful spectacle,
" almost a skeleton," was carried on board a twenty-
gun frigate in the mouth of the Hugli. H.M.S. *Dolphin*
sailed for Portsmouth, blue days at sea succeeded one
another, and gradually (entirely, in his opinion, owing
to the kindness of Captain Pigot), Horatio Nelson,
aged seventeen, realised that he was not to die this
time. But with his convalescence from what was
apparently malaria came dreadful mental depression.
" My mind was staggered with a view of the difficulties
I had to surmount, and the little interest I possessed.
I could discover no means of reaching the object of
my ambition." He recounted the anecdote a quarter
of a century later, on an after-dinner walk with an
antiquarian in the pleasure grounds of a Welsh castle,
but for many years that redoubtable character,
Captain Thomas Masterman Hardy, had been perfectly familiar with his Chief's belief in " the radiant
orb " which urged him onward to renown. Its first
appearance was after " a long and gloomy reverie "

in his cot in the *Dolphin*, when the spirits of a good
clergyman's son had reached such a low ebb that " I
almost wished myself overboard." A couple of years
before he had been noted as " a boy with a florid
countenance, rather stout and athletic." If this
impression was correct, it was a good advertisement
for going to sea young, for certainly as a child he had
been fair and fragile. He was never again to be
anything but pale and little, and his hair, originally
a rich auburn, was hereafter to be so light as to require
little powder. In the blessed rise of spirits which
followed his hour of darkness and desertion, " a
sudden glow of patriotism was kindled within me,
and presented my King and Country as my patron.
My mind exulted in the idea. ' Well, then,' I exclaimed, ' I will be a hero, and confiding in Providence,
I will brave every danger.' "

II

Influence and interest were of first importance in
the eighteenth century. The young officer without a
patron had a hard row to hoe. The words occur con-
stantly in the early letters of Horatio Nelson. He
returned home from the East Indies to find that his
" influence " had improved during his absence. His
uncle, Captain Maurice Suckling, had become Comptroller of the Navy. When he presented himself for
his examination as Lieutenant, the Comptroller,
Chairman of the officers assembled, gave no sign of

recognition. Only after the young Nelson had acquitted himself well did Captain Suckling beg leave to introduce his nephew. " I did not wish the younker to be favoured. I felt convinced he would pass a good examination, and you see, gentlemen, I have not been disappointed." In fact, the younker's family background was as reassuring as his professional record.

The Nelsons had been established in East Anglia as clergy, for two generations. They came of sound Yorkshire stock, small landowners, farmers, graziers. . . . Both the boy's grandfathers had been in holy orders; his father, two of his great-uncles, eight cousins and two of his brothers followed suit. On the mother's side he could claim something more distinguished. " Your titled relations," as his father called them, were headed by the Walpoles, and Horatio, second Baron, of Wolterton, had stood sponsor and bestowed his name at the christening of the sixth infant of the Rector of Burnham Thorpe. Time was to show that the Walpoles, as patrons, were totally useless, but two of Mrs. Nelson's brothers were to fulfil every expectation. They came down to the stone-cold Rectory for the funeral of their poor sister, which took place when the boy Horace (as he was always called) was nine years old. Mr. William Suckling, an official in the Customs and Navy Office, promised to find an opening for one nephew: Captain Maurice Suckling would take one to sea. Only three of the Rector's eleven children had died in infancy. As soon as young Maurice, his eldest son, was fifteen, he was

sent off to Mr. William Suckling, to become a clerk.
He meekly pursued for the rest of his life, an occu-
pation which he found uncongenial and was often
obliged to his brother Horace for settling his affairs.
Captain Suckling did not get the boy whom he expected. William, large and robustious, came next on
the list. Horace and he had begun their education
at the Royal Grammar School, Norwich, and passed
on together to Sir William Paston's School, North
Walsham. During the Christmas holidays of 1770-1
while the Rector was attempting to assuage his rheu-
matism by a course of Bath waters, the boys read in
the local newspaper that, in view of war with Spain,
H.M.S. *Raisonnable* (Captain Suckling) was being
recommissioned. " Do, brother William, write to my
father at Bath, and tell him I should like to go to
my Uncle Maurice to sea." William and the Rector
obeyed, and a hearty sea-officer replied characteristi-
cally. " What has poor Horace done, who is so weak,
that he above all the rest should be sent to rough it
out at sea? But let him come; and the first time we
go into action, a cannon-ball may knock off his head,
and provide for him at once."

The Rector and his sailor son set off for London on
a March morning of 1771, a highly ingenuous couple.
The Rev. Edward Nelson was a tall, awkwardly-built
man, with shoulder-long prematurely white hair and
large myopic brown eyes. He had ideas ahead of his
time, for instance, that all the girls should have pro-
fessions, as well as the boys; he was an exemplary

parish priest, and something of a rosarian. But he was essentially unpractical. After undertaking the long expensive journey from King's Lynn to London, to deliver his twelve-year-old son, he failed in the last lap. He put the lad on the stage-coach for Chatham, and returned sadly to the handsome, new-built, red-brick Kentish Town mansion of Mr. William Suckling. Horatio Nelson never forgot the first day of his naval career. Nobody expected him at Chatham. He identified the *Raisonnable* lying in the Medway, but could not find anyone to take him out to her. But for a benevolent unknown officer who bent to hear the name of Captain Suckling, the chilled and straying waif would have gone hungry. When he reached the *Raisonnable* he paced her decks alone. Captain Suckling was not in his ship, and nobody had heard of his nephew.

From internal evidence it appears that Nelson did not escape the miseries of the midshipmen's berth at a date when these were remarkable. (He once, when Commander-in-Chief in the Mediterranean, opened conversation with a tongue-tied youngster by remarking, " You entered the Service at a very early age to have been in the action of Cape St. Vincent," and when he heard " Eleven years, my lord," looked grave, and muttered, " Much too young.") But a kindly uncle looked after him as far as possible. He was sent to the West Indies, in a merchant vessel, and returned, " a practical seaman," to undertake small-boat work—was allowed to handle the cutter of the

Triumph guardship, and even the decked long-boat.
" By degrees " he learned to become " confident of
myself amongst rocks and sands." His uncle did not
dissuade him when he volunteered for a Polar expedition which was stopped by ice north of Hakluyt
Headland, reached the Seven Islands and discovered
Walden Island; and Captain Lutwidge of H.M.S.
Carcass, in after years, often entertained guests with
his tale of Horatio Nelson defying a " bruin " on an
ice-flow. When a squadron was fitted out under Sir
Edward Hughes, for the East Indies, the Comptroller
recommended his nephew, and Captain George
Farmer of H.M.S. *Seahorse*, finding him " extremely
attentive to his duties when stationed in the foretop
at watch and ward," rated him midshipman. But
after eighteen months visiting every port from Bengal
to Bushire, malaria struck down a promising naval
aspirant.

III

Two days after he passed his examination, he received
his commission as Second Lieutenant of the *Lowestoffe*
frigate (Captain Locker) and wrote in high spirits to
his brother William, " So I am now left in World to
shift for myself, which I hope to do so as to bring
Credit to myself and Friends." He went off for Jamaica
in such haste that he left behind, unfinished, in the
studio of Mr. Rigaud, his portrait in uniform.

His connection with Locker did not last very long,

a little over two years, but this excellent man, who
was one of the first to recognise his quality, remained
a lifelong friend, and must be regarded as his sea-
daddy. He gave Nelson command of the *Lowestoffe's*
tender (" even a frigate was not sufficiently active for
my mind "), and in the *Little Lucy* schooner, named
after Miss Locker, Nelson made himself " a complete
pilot for all the passages through the islands situated
on the north side Hispaniola."

On her second cruise from Jamaica, in foul November weather, the *Lowestoffe* overhauled an American
letter of marque. A heavy sea was running, and the
First Lieutenant of the frigate failed to board the prize.
Locker, seeing a boat still lying alongside in imminent
danger of being swamped, shouted, " Have I no
officer in this ship who can board the prize? "
The Master of the *Lowestoffe* found himself fore-
stalled at the gangway by the Second Lieutenant
(" It is my turn now, and if I come back, it is yours "),
and Nelson did return triumphant. But he was so
long absent that Locker was anxious. This " little
incident," which he justly believed to presage his
character, stuck in Nelson's memory, and when, at
the request of the editor of the *Naval Chronicle*, he
supplied notes for a biography (scribbled during the
course of a court martial at Port Mahon in 1799), he
included it. It therefore became the subject of a large
dramatic oil-painting.

Captain Locker, before he retired home " to peace
and plenty," mentioned his Second Lieutenant to Sir

Peter Parker, and this Chief took Nelson into his flagship, where he soon rose to be First. The West Indies
stations were famous, even in time of peace, for rapid
promotion, and war with France had now opened. At
the age of twenty Nelson found himself appointed
Commander of the *Badger* brig, detailed to protect
the north side of Jamaica, and being " pretty successful " in taking prizes. A note of confidence entered
his letters home (" I never allow inferiors to dictate ").
His first experience of fire at sea belonged to this
period, and he thought that, too, worthy of mention.
Two hours after H.M.S. *Glasgow* came into Montego
Bay on a June evening, smoke, followed by flames,
began to stream towards the sunset skies. A steward,
stealing rum, had upset a light amongst the liquor
casks. Her crew were saved mainly owing to the
prompt action of the *Badger*. Nelson came up with his
boats, ordered the men of the doomed frigate to cast
their powder overboard and point their guns skyward
before leaping overboard, and rescued every man.

He was rising in the Service with as much rapidity
as even he could have hoped, but his relief was
enormous when, three months before he came of age,
Parker posted him to the *Hinchingbrooke* frigate. For
his news from home was that his uncle could do no
more for him. The Comptroller's last words to the
Rev. Edmund Nelson had been that the Rector would
live to see Horace an Admiral. In a very old Will
he had left every nephew five hundred pounds, and
Mr. William Suckling was going to give " poor

Horace" a naval heirloom, the dress-sword of Captain Galfridus Walpole, who had lost his right arm in an action against the French in 1711. Captain Nelson replied that he would always remember Captain Suckling with gratitude. "I feel myself to my country, his heir." Further promotion could come to him by seniority only; no junior officer could now be passed over his head; but he realised that so far he had been lucky.

Meanwhile, chances of distinction seemed promising. Jamaica expected invasion daily, and Nelson, in charge of the batteries at Fort Royal, attended by red-coats and negroes, looked out eagerly for the Comte D'Estaing. But the French admiral sailed on from Haiti to Savannah, and after a three-months' cruise, which brought him about £800 prize-money, Nelson jumped at the offer that he should go as senior naval officer on a joint expedition. Its object was much more impressive than the numbers employed, and even he considered "how it will turn out, God knows." It had in fact been sent at the wrong season, and "Yellow Jack," the dreaded fever particularly rife all round the Caribbean, was to frustrate it. But his fancy was touched by the story of "a river which none but the Spaniards since the time of the buccaneers had ever ascended," and when he had convoyed the troops to the mouth of the San Juan, he discovered that no one had any idea of the position or strength of the forts which they must attack as a first step towards "the capture of the rich cities of Grenada and Leon and a passage to the Pacific." " A light-haired boy came to me in a little frigate," reported the officer in command of the military. " In two or three days he displayed himself, and afterwards he directed all the operations." Two of the *Hinchingbrooke's* boats, and Nelson, went with the troops, ammunition and siege-train landed, and entered upon a continued night-mare. The boat work was appallingly difficult, for the river contained very little water in the lower reaches, and in the upper unsuspected rapids. Over many stretches, tropical vegetation grew so thickly that even at noon the scene was illuminated by no more than an uncanny chequered green twilight. Sweating pig-tailed marines, seamen, and soldiers, who got wet through repeatedly, began to suffer from blinding headaches, which they attributed to the glare from the white sand of the district. Overhead, monkeys mocked their toil and labour; and the bite of the local snake produced, they averred, death followed by putrefaction before a stretcher party had found the victim. Nevertheless, by the time that their next trial, the rains, descended upon them, they had captured a fortified island from which the Spanish garrison had fled on their approach, ascended the river nearly a hundred miles, and come in sight of Fort San Juan.

Nelson continued on duty, " made batteries and fought them," although already smitten by the sick-ness which was to carry off all but ten of the *Hinching-brooke's* detachment of two hundred men. He was recalled to Port Royal just in time to save his life, but was too ill to take up his appointment to H.M.S. *Janus*, " a very fine frigate." He never would allow that the San Juan expedition had been futile and ill-conceived. If it had been sent at the right time it might have succeeded. It was his first experience of a combined operation, and dear to him—a tragedy not a failure.

On his return home he took a three-months' course of treatment at Bath, " carried to and from bed with the most excruciating tortures," and was touched by the speech of a fashionable physician who presented him with a very small bill. " Pray, Captain Nelson, allow me to follow what I consider my professional duty. Your illness, sir, was brought on by serving your King and Country, and believe me I love both too well to be able to receive any more." Nelson's duty took him hobbling into the Admiralty when he was scarcely yet able to walk. His next ship, the *Albemarle*, was never a good sailer, and eventually he came to the sad conclusion that her first owners, the French, must have taught her to run away. He spent the winter of 1781-2 being " frozen for a season " employed in convoy service in the North Sea, and then was ordered to America. For the first and last time in his life, during a cruise from Quebec, he and his ship's company developed scurvy. Thereafter, fresh vegetables and lemon juice were with him articles of faith. He fell in love with " Fair Canada " and with a fair Canadian, Miss Mary Simpson, aged sixteen, but was restrained from making her an offer of marriage by an enigmatic figure destined to become his prize-agent and his closest personal friend outside the Service. Alexander Davison, a merchant and ship-owner of Northumbrian descent, went to jail twice in Nelson's lifetime. The first occasion was connected with electioneering, and was capable of being passed off as an accident that might have happened to any gentleman; but a Parliamentary committee of inquiry took a more serious view of his conduct as a Government contractor. Davison, who in the days of his splendour behaved with flamboyant generosity, always con-gratulated himself on having prevented Nelson from wrecking his career by an imprudent early marriage. For Nelson, on his arrival at Sandy Hook, where he found twelve battle-scarred ships-of-the-line under Lord Hood, at once made a favourable impression on that great veteran, by asking boldly for " a better ship and a better station." The young officer had been told, " You are come on a fine station for making prize-money," but his reply had been, " Yes, sir, but the West Indies is the station for honour." At twenty-four, his appearance was still extraordinarily youthful. Prince William Henry (afterwards William IV, and a trusty but not useful friend) had the watch on deck when the *Albemarle's* barge came alongside Lord Hood's flagship. The royal midshipman was equally astonished by the old-fashioned uniform and vivid personality of " the merest boy of a Captain I ever beheld."

Nelson did not see the service for which he had

hoped under Hood's flag. Spain and America made peace, and the *Albemarle* was paid off. He betook himself to the Continent to learn French, but got no farther than St. Omer, where he fell in love again. The Christian name of the incomparable Miss Andrews has never come to light, but by the time that he sailed for the Leeward Isles, in command of the *Boreas* frigate, he described himself as " crossed in love and done with politics." An effort to get himself adopted as a candidate in the General Election of 1784 had been a mortifying experience.

It was as the Captain of the *Boreas*, on Sunday, March 11th, 1787, that he pledged himself to be faithful till death to Mrs. Frances Nisbet, a widow a few months his senior. The wedding took place, according to the fashion of the day, in the drawing-room of a private house—Montpelier, Nevis—and Prince William Henry, who had insisted that he should give the bride away, found her pretty and sensible and likely to have a great deal of money if her uncle, the Governor of the island, saw fit. She was the mother of a passionate-looking black-browed boy of six, whom the confident Nelson intended to treat just like his own children. " Poor Nelson is over head and ears in love . . . He is now in for it." He was indeed. None of the bright hopes voiced on that spring day were to be fulfilled. All his life he was to complain of two things—cold and poverty. He was now going home to a cold hearth, with a cold woman, and he was to die in debt.

IV

He had been the bane of poor ineffectual Admiral Sir Richard Hughes. The *dossier* of his service in the Leeward Isles included a long list of complaints from important residents. They had found their irregular trading with American craft suppressed by a strange young officer without interest or influence. He had refused to be daunted by having writs for damages to the tune of £4,000 served upon him, and he had proceeded to expose the peculations of many eminent officials of the dockyard.

His five years " on the beach " from 1787-1793 were almost entirely miserable. Mr. and Mrs. Horatio Nelson, pressed by the saintly old Rector of Burnham Thorpe to make their home with him, did so rather from necessity than choice. The Parsonage House was pulled down during Nelson's lifetime, but many engravings of the birthplace of a hero attest that it may have been picturesque enough in summer, but must have been a penance in winter. Mrs. Nelson, always ailing, took to bed for days together. Nelson occupied himself with making a model ship-of-the-line and digging in the garden. He read much, and spent many hours of candlelight with nautical charts, and in addressing letters to their lordships, begging for employment. He never failed to leave his name at Lord Hood's door, when he performed the journey " upwards of 120 miles " to London, and he got a shock when the Admiral who had " found " him

finally said that he could not ask the First Lord for a ship for Captain Nelson. " The King was impressed with an unfavourable opinion of me." A note in the hand of his wife tells that Nelson " once spoke of the Russian service." In France, the Bastille had fallen, and Louis XVI and Marie-Antoinette had been forcibly escorted by their subjects to residence in Paris. Nelson, reading the newspapers diligently, refused to despair. " Neither at sea nor on shore, through the caprice of a Minister, can my attachment to my King be shaken. That will never end but with my life."

Most unfortunately, his elegant bride from the West Indies scorned all his family. Jolly Mrs. Bolton, Susanna, who was the mother of twins, and many more, and the wife of a merchant (" in a prosperous way of trade in corn, malt, coals, etc.") had served as a milliner's assistant in a Bath shop before she met her Sam. Poor Maurice undoubtedly made calls upon Horatio's purse. William, now in holy orders, was by all accounts a great trencherman and always unblushingly on the make. But his handwriting was that of a scholar, and Horatio loved him. Edmund, who had failed in business as a linen draper, died of a decline during the Horatio Nelsons' long stay in the old home. Suckling, who had also made an unlucky business venture, might, his father hoped, after taking his degree at Cambridge, be ordained, and " pass amongst a crowd of undistinguished preachers." Catherine, " Kitty," the flower of the flock, had made

a fairy-tale love-match and lived in ease and affluence with a husband handsome, travelled and rich. But Mrs. Horatio Nelson refused to join in the chorus of praise that surrounded Mr. George Matcham. She thought him the most unsettled man she had ever met.

When Nelson learnt, on January 7th, 1793, that he was to get a ship at last, and his first of-the-line, his joy was unbounded. " *Post nubila Phoebus*," he wrote to his wife. " Your son will explain the motto. After clouds come sunshine. The Admiralty so smile upon me that I am as much surprised as when they frowned." England was going to war with France again, and this war was to last his lifetime and ten years more. At the Admiralty the name of Captain Horatio Nelson was looked upon with a new eye.

H.M.S. *Agamemnon* (64) went down the river from Chatham on a mid-March day. Her ship's company included a number of Norfolk volunteers (worth two of other men, in her Captain's opinion), and he was also taking to sea with him three little sons of East Anglian clergymen, and his own step-son, aged twelve. As the *Agamemnon* approached the Nore with exhilarating speed, Master Nisbet began to suffer, but he was reported to his mother as having been only " a little seasick." Nelson had not yet reached the age when he made no secret of the fact that all his life he was haunted by miserable, repeated and incurable sea-sickness.

2

"Old Mediterranean Man"

A<small>T DAWN</small> on September 12th, 1793, Nelson finished
a letter to his wife " begun off the Island of Sardinia
and finished at anchor, off Naples." He had been
sent by Hood to bring up a convoy of Neapolitan
troops to assist the allies occupying Toulon. " My
poor fellows have not had a morsel of fresh meat or
vegetables for near nineteen weeks, and in that time
I have only had my foot twice on shore, at Cadiz.
We are absolutely sick with fatigue." He was fast
becoming what he called an " old Mediterranean
man," and was to be eternally on the wing for the
next three years, in search of glory. But far from
sounding jaded, his long dutiful epistle to a lady in
lodgings at Swaffham, who mourned that the lot of
a sailor's wife was hard, was remarkable for a keyed-up
expectant note. He described Vesuvius, lighting a
scene of operatic beauty, as his worn ship came slowly
into a famous bay. He fretted that he might be
missing chances of action by being sent off on a mission
which might fail. His postscript was breathless—
" We are in the Bay, all night, becalmed, and nothing
could be finer than the view of Mount Vesuvius."

Next day he entered upon negotiations which were an unqualified success. The Queen of Naples (whom he did not mention in his letters home from the British Embassy) was a sister of the murdered Marie-Antoinette. The King, a swarthy, oafish monarch, devoted to the chase, promised without hesitation six thousand of his best troops. The Prime Minister, Sir John Acton, was an Englishman, another happy chance. The British Envoy and Minister Pleni-potentiary, Sir William Hamilton, aristocrat and antiquarian, who had almost lost hope of playing a leading part in the diplomatic field, appeared to the visiting sea-captain the embodiment of a grand seig-neur. Everyone in the Fleet knew that Lady Hamilton, who was young enough to be his daughter, had been Sir William's mistress, and that the homely house-keeper at the Embassy, who passed by the name of Mrs. Cadogan, was her ladyship's mother. Nelson had taken Josiah with him, and the midshipman rather than the Captain fell to the lot of a hostess of capti-vating appearance and manners during a four-days' stay. " Lady Hamilton has been wonderfully kind and good to Josiah. She is a young woman of amiable manners, and who does honour to the station to which she is raised."

News that a French man-of-war was on the coast of Sardinia sent the *Agamemnon* to sea at two hours' notice, and he did not see Naples or the Hamiltons again for five years. But he corresponded with Sir William, and sent Lady Hamilton respectful thanks for

having remembered her promise to send him views of
Naples.

II

He had " a little brush " with an enemy squadron
of four frigates on his passage to join Commodore
Linzee at Cagliari, and had not the wind failed, must
have taken the *Melpomene* of forty guns.   But the
Agamemnon's rigging was so much cut up that she was
not able, without a small refit, to enter upon further
action; and the *Melpomene's* consorts brought her, in
an almost sinking state, into Calvi.   Satisfaction in the
Agamemnon, however, after her first engagement, was
general, and William Hoste, midshipman, wrote home
to Norfolk sentiments which were to become very
familiar.   " Captain Nelson is acknowledged one of
the first characters in the Service, and is universally
beloved by his men and officers."   Hood, on hearing
of the affair, gave Nelson a detached command
(" most handsome ") and empowered him to deal
with the frigates which had escaped him.   All were in
Corsican ports, and it soon appeared that Corsica
must be captured as a base of operations.   The troops
at Hood's disposal had never been sufficient to control
the land defences of Toulon, and when Republican
artillery, under the command of Lieutenant-Colonel
Buonaparte, gained command of the roadstead, the
British Admiral dryly informed his allies (of six
nationalities) that he was about to order his Fleet to

sea, taking with it as many Royalist French ships as were ready to sail and setting fire to the rest. Nelson stoutly proclaimed the evacuation of Toulon was " for England, a most happy event," and after San Fiorenzo had been taken, without much difficulty, he begged Hood to allow him to " anchor and act with the army " in besieging Bastia. Co-operation between the Navy and the Army was at a very low ebb, and General Dundas flatly refused, before the arrival of reinforcements from Gibraltar, to proceed to the attack. The force with which Nelson landed consisted of about fourteen hundred men—seamen, and marines, or soldiers doing duty as marines—and although he had reconnoitred Bastia as thoroughly as possible, it was soon evident that his reports as to her defence and garrison had been optimistic. Corsican patriots watched with amazement while Norfolk seamen made roads, hauled up their guns, and cut down the fragrant undergrowth known as the " maquis " on their advance towards the Camponella redoubt. Enemy grape-shot and musketry did their work, and Nelson himself received a " sharp cut in the back." Nearly six weeks passed before the Bastia garrison, short of food and ammunition, and terrified of falling into the hands of victorious natives, sent in a flag of truce; and to Nelson's exasperation the army, from San Fiorenzo, arrived just in time to make a triumphal entry. He commented, " I may truly say this has been a Naval Expedition," but hoped " we shall now join heart and hand against Calvi."

Calvi, from the first, appeared a much tougher nut to crack than Bastia, but General the Hon. Charles Stuart, a man about whom there were only two opinions—he was either loved or hated—possessed all the " activity " desired by Nelson. From the moment he arrived to say that he was anxious to get on with the attack if Captain Nelson thought fit to proceed with the shipping (" I certainly do "), they took to one another. Calvi, a picturesque antique town, perched on beetling crags above malarial lagoons, was well garrisoned, and protected by the star-shaped fort, Muzello. Stuart and Nelson anchored, after some difficulty, opposite a cove known as Porto Agro, went ashore, and were disappointed to find that no better or nearer place was to be discovered in which to land their guns and stores. They examined the enemy outposts, and reluctantly decided that Porto Agro, three and a half miles west of their object, must be their base. Nelson repeated that Lord Hood would be in the offing to protect them from the French Fleet at Golfe Juan, and disembarkation began. A Corsican thunderstorm of the first quality opened while they were still getting field-pieces and military baggage ashore, and it lasted for twenty-four hours. Most of the ships were obliged to put to sea, and from Martello Bay, Hood contemplated helplessly a force which had believed itself " under his wing," deserted on a hostile shore. But throughout the thunder and lightning, gale and downpour, Nelson's seamen began to repeat the prodigies which they had performed at Bastia,

" dragging cannon up steep mountains, and carrying shot and shell to batteries built, armed and manned under his personal supervision." Gradually, he got boats off, through the surf, to such ships as were visible; rations, powder and shot were brought in, and guns began to pass up towards Fort Monteciusco, close to the south-west of the town.

When Captain Serocold of the Royal Navy was killed " by a grape-shot passing through his head as he cheered the people who were dragging the gun," Nelson seized a moment to scribble a line to his ever-anxious Fanny, who might see in the newspaper that a sea-officer had fallen, and conclude that she must be the widow.

" I am very busy, yet own I am in all my glory. Except with you, I would not be anywhere but where I am, for the world. I am well aware my poor services will not be noticed; I have no interest; but however services may be received, it is not right in an Officer to slacken his zeal for his Country."

There never was such a place for bitterness and jealousies as Corsica. The native taste for vendetta seemed to have communicated itself to the British Navy and Army. Nelson was sore when Hood's despatch " put me where I never was—in the rear," and believed that his outstanding leadership had been more appreciated by Sir Gilbert Elliot, the newly-appointed Viceroy of the island, and Stuart, " a stranger and a landsman." The sea-officer sent home with the despatch had never been on a battery, and the Artillery lieutenant singled out for praise, promoted to a Company and appointed an aide-de-camp to Stuart, seemed to Nelson (who had commended him) to be giving himself airs. "There is nothing like kicking down the ladder a man rises by."

The enemy, perceiving the British arriving with guns over mountains deemed inaccessible, began to open heavy and concentrated fire upon their works, and on the morning of July 12th, 1794, Nelson was struck with great violence, in the face and breast by splinters, stones and sand from the *merlon* of a battery hit by an enemy shell. The cheerful, hard-drinking young surgeon who performed his first dressing promised him that his wounded eye should recover a measure of sight, and in his daily report to Hood he mentioned, "I got a little hurt this morning; not much as you may judge from my writing." The siege was proceeding steadily but he was beginning to be reminded of San Juan. "We have more to fear from the Climate than the Enemy." Seamen who had worked barefoot, dragging field-pieces up roads built by themselves, had mounted the guns under fire, fought them, and slept on the batteries with pikes and cutlasses always ready, were beginning to report sick in alarming numbers.

The expedition against Calvi lasted almost two months, and the result was a near-run thing. The garrison had heard of the pestilence in the English camp, and held out to the last possible moment.

Hood and Stuart were both stricken, and Nelson was beginning to suffer from more than agony from his eye, when at last the white flag was visible, drooping from the star fort, lit by the glare of the famous Corsican " Lion Sun." Amongst the spoils of war relinquished in the port was the *Melpomene*, " the most beautiful frigate I ever saw."

It was in the sick-bay of Hood's flagship, H.M.S. *Victory*, that Nelson learnt for certain what he had guessed a month past. The pupil of his right eye was now large, irregular in shape, and immovable. As he had been absent from the battery only a few hours, his name had never appeared in the casualty list, a fact which was to cause him much future annoyance. He now confessed to his wife the extent of his " slight scratch," and assured her that " the blemish is nothing: not to be perceived, unless told." It had never kept him from his duty. He said that nothing short of the loss of a limb would have done that.

III

Corsica, that grave of reputations, was now reduced. Sir Gilbert Elliot went into residence at Bastia, and Hood sailed for home, leaving the command with Admiral William Hotham. The *Agamemnon*, continuing with the Fleet, distinguished herself in two minor engagements in March and July, 1795, which were greeted as victories, but scorned by Nelson as miserably conducted. " The scrambling distant fire was a farce." From the Palazzo Sessa, Sir William Hamilton wrote gently, " I can perceive, *entre nous*, that my old friend Hotham is not quite awake enough for such a command as that of the King's Fleet in the Mediterranean."

Nelson's letters from his wife were sad reading, and he answered them with unwonted sharpness. (" Why you should be uneasy about me so as to make yourself ill, I know not . . . The Service must ever supersede all private considerations.") It was clear to him that after a period of eclipse his reputation was increasing, and he had not yet seen a Fleet action. He was filled with hope when he was ordered to take command of a frigate squadron in the Gulf of Genoa, and co-operate with the Austrian Army, under General Baron de Vins. But troubles began to thicken about him. The news that Hood had been superseded, and was not coming out again, caused him anger and grief. Hood had kept his promise of recommending him, but Lord Spencer, who had now succeeded Lord Chatham at the Admiralty, would, in Hood's opinion, be likely to mark with indifference and inattention all applications from a Chief to whom he had never spoken since ordering him to strike his flag. De Vins, a courtly old gentleman, who began by announcing that he expected to lead his troops into Nice within six weeks, soon perceiving that Hotham had sent him a few frigates much in need of a refit, in charge of a highly exhausting young man in the same condition, prudently decided not to do anything rash. He apologised to Nelson that " the politics of his court so continually tied his hands," and produced schemes which entailed " a small degree of assistance from Admiral Hotham," whom Nelson could not persuade to appear. The *Agamemnon*, after months of ceaseless vigilance, was nearly as crank as her Captain, and Nelson had personal worries. His servant, Frank Lepee, a popular figure with his family, was drinking. Frank, who had followed him up the San Juan, would have to go, and he had no one obvious as a replacement. Tom Allen, who had volunteered from Burnham Thorpe, was mighty pleased when he found himself promoted what he called " wally-de-sham." He was a dreadful-looking specimen, with profuse lank black hair, stunted, uncouth, entirely illiterate. But he knew not fear, and he did not drink. Nelson endured him for seven years.

For ten days, in August, Nelson was almost blind, and in great pain. His " good " eye was beginning to give out, and he kept on waking o' nights feeling " as if a girth were buckled taut over my breast." In November military events began to move, but not in the right direction. He regretted that the *Agamemnon* could not be cut in two. The British Minister at Genoa was calling frantically for her return, so he laid her across the harbour's mouth, in very bad weather. But he knew that by leaving Vado Bay he had given enemy gunboats their chance of plaguing the Austrian left flank. By December 4th he noted the end of a sad story. " The Austrians, by all accounts, did not stand firm. The French, half-naked, were determined to conquer or die. General de Vins, from ill-health, he says, gave up the command in the middle of the battle, and from that moment not a soldier stayed at his post . . . Thus has ended my campaign." The French had captured Vado Bay. He had never thought much of it as a base. Hotham had retired to Naples, and Sir Hyde Parker, in temporary command, had deprived him of all but one frigate of " my Squadron." Nelson sailed for Leghorn, to refit, full of anxiety. If he fell in with the enemy fleet said to be ready for sea at Toulon, and with troops embarked, he thought his situation would be very precarious. " My Ship and Ship's Company are worn out, but folks at Home do not feel for us." But folks at home were beginning to hear of him. An article in the *Gentleman's Magazine* was soon to record that men of a certain ship of sixty-four guns in the Mediterranean called the *Bellerophon* the " Bully Ruffian," the *Polyphemus*, " Polly Infamous," and their own *Agamemnon*, " Eggs and Bacon."

He had an undisturbed passage to the free and neutral Tuscan port, and there heard with great interest of the arrival from Spithead of a new Chief. The appointment of Sir John Jervis, " who I understand is a man of business," was welcome to him, but by no means all in the Fleet were so pleased at the prospect of an Admiral with an unsparing tongue and a very sharp nose for inefficiency. Nelson had met him once, years past. The scene was a perfect little eighteenth-century *vignette*. In the dark Treasury Passage of the House of Commons, Jervis, Member for Yarmouth, had recognised an old messmate from Captain Locker's habit of using an eye-glass fitted to the head of his cane. Locker had hastened to present his young élève, Captain Horatio Nelson.

Nelson emerged from his first duty call upon his new Chief with so satisfied a mien that a soured brother-officer burst out, " You did just as you pleased in Lord Hood's time, the same in Admiral Hotham's, and now again with Sir John Jervis! " He got a " pretty strong answer." Jervis, after accepting Captain Locker's kind remembrances, had at once made Nelson the offer of the *St. George* (80) or *Zealous* (74), and unruffled by a refusal of either, had proceeded to ask his knowledge and even advice on several matters upon which others in the Fleet should, in Nelson's opinion, have been better able to inform him. Six weeks later, Midshipman Hoste wrote home to Norfolk from the *Agamemnon*: " Our squadron at present consists of two Sail-of-the-Line and four Frigates, but is to be increased in the summer, when we shall not want for amusement, I make no doubt, as our Commodore does not like to be idle.

" I suppose your curiosity is excited by the word *Commodore* Nelson. It gives me infinite pleasure to be able to relieve it by informing you that our good Captain has had this additional mark of distinction conferred upon him, which, I dare say you will agree with me, his merit richly deserves. His Broad Pendant is now flying; therefore I must beg my dear father to draw an additional cork."

The end of a chapter came in July, 1796, when Commodore Nelson moved into the *Captain* (74). Orders had come for the worst ship-of-the-line to go home with a convoy, and there was no doubt that he must part with the *Agamemnon*. Her ground tier was giving way; even he admitted that her appearance was that of " a tub floating on the water." Yet, as he watched her disappear into the midsummer haze, from Fiorenzo Bay, with his very handsome attentive new First Lieutenant, Mr. Edward Berry, alert by his side, he could not help remarking that although the *Diadem* (another 64) was certainly in better plight, in point of sailing the old *Agamemnon* had the superiority.

His promotion made little change in the service in which he was employed. His itinerary was Golfe Juan (always " Gourjean " to him), Genoa, Leghorn, Porto Ferrajo in Elba, and the Corsican ports. His duty was blockade, and harassing enemy movements on shore. He reported without comment a succession of French military victories. General Buonaparte had beaten the Allies at Montenotte, Millesimo, Dega and Lodi. He had ridden into Milan on a little white horse. His troops took Leghorn so suddenly that a number of important English residents and tourists only just got away in time. Lady Elliot, wife of the Viceroy of Corsica, embarked without anything except the clothes she happened to be wearing when Captain Thomas Fremantle appeared to rush her

down side-streets to the frigate *Dolphin*. To the amusement of the Fleet, Jervis took into his own flagship
another English refugee family rescued by Fremantle,
which included two muslin-clad, curly-headed young
ladies. The Misses Wynne kept Journals, invaluable to
biographers of Nelson, but needless to say, as Miss Betsy
Wynne (who soon lost her heart to Fremantle) was
seventeen, Admiral Jervis (aged 62) and Commodore
Nelson (38) appeared in her pages as just " old."

Nelson arrived at the Viceroy's palace at Bastia on
the night of September 29th, in hot haste. He had
been sent down from Leghorn to protect Corsica from
a French landing. On opening the instructions awaiting him at Bastia, he had received a shock. Jervis had
been informed of the Cabinet decision to " withdraw
the blessings of the British Constitution from the
people of Corsica," and the British Fleet from the
Mediterranean. Northern Italy was completely sub-
jugated, neutrality had been forced on Naples, and
the large but rotten fleet of Spain was now joined to
that of France. Jervis looked forward to an early
meeting with the Spaniards, but to Nelson orders to
conduct the evacuation of Corsica were " sackcloth
and ashes," and that the Fleet should quit the Mediterranean seemed to him disgraceful. " They at home
do not know what the Fleet is capable of performing
—anything and everything. Of all Fleets I ever saw,
I never beheld one, in point of officers and men, equal
to Sir John Jervis's, who is a Commander-in-Chief to
lead them to glory."

He stood for Elba, with a fine wind, a fortnight later, having, much to the surprise of General de Burgh, successfully embarked all the garrison, with their stores, guns and provisions. There had been, according to the General, as many hostile Corsicans as British troops in the citadel, but " Commodore Nelson, by the firm tone he held, soon reduced these gentlemen to order." It was exasperating, when he got to Gibraltar, to learn that he must return to Elba, and bring away the troops from that island. He scribbled a line to his wife. " I am going on a most important Mission, which with God's blessing I have little doubt of accomplishing. It is not a fighting Mission, therefore do not be anxious." But it was to be a fighting mission. Off Cartagena, amongst fresh gales and cloudy weather, with his flag in the *Minerve* frigate, and the *Blanche* in company, he fell in with the Spanish *Santa Sabina* and *Ceres*. The *Santa Sabina*, engaged by the *Minerve*, after losing her mizzen mast, her main and fore-mast and having a hundred and sixty-four men killed or wounded, struck, and received a prize-crew on board. The *Ceres*, engaged by the *Blanche*, also struck, but before she could be taken in tow, a Spanish squadron of two of-the-line and two frigates came in sight and action recommenced. " We very nearly escaped visiting a Spanish prison." The *Santa Sabina* and *Ceres* were retaken, and Nelson sadly wrote a letter in the high style of old chivalrous days to the Captain-General of Cartagena, offering to exchange the Captain of the *Santa Sabina* for the two lieutenants sent by him on board the Spanish frigates in command of prize-crews. One of them bore the name of Hardy.

He reached Porto Ferrajo on Christmas Eve, to find the place *en fête*, and when he entered the Theatre, where a military Ball was in progress, the band, much to his surprise, struck up " See the Conquering Hero Comes," followed by " Rule Britannia." In his chagrin at losing his prizes, he had forgotten that the action in which he had just taken part would find a place in the *Gazette*, " and I may venture to say, it was what I know the English like."

He had a tussle with de Burgh lasting nearly a month. The General wanted written orders from the Horse Guards before he retired with his troops to Lisbon and Gibraltar. The arrival of the ex-Viceroy of Corsica, who had been on a diplomatic tour to Rome and Naples, did not simplify the situation, for Sir Gilbert Elliot warily refused to supply the documents suggested by de Burgh. At last, Sir Gilbert went on board the *Minerve* philosophically, and Nelson, who was on tenterhooks lest he should be missing a Fleet action under the flag of Jervis, left de Burgh sufficient transports to remove his troops in three days, and a small escort, and washed his hands of him.

In order to bring Jervis the latest news of the enemy, it had been his intention to look in at Toulon, Mahon and Cartagena. The wind was foul for Mahon, so he cut Minorca out of his programme. From Cartagena he hurried. The news there was that the Spanish Fleet had left that port. At Gibraltar he learnt that

it had passed the Rock to the westward, and that
Jervis had taken up his station off Cadiz. He went in
to Rosia Bay to pick up the lieutenants and prize-crews
taken in the *Santa Sabina*, and as he came out perceived two Spanish sail-of-the-line and a frigate
awaiting him. They began to chase him, and the
order to clear for action was given. Colonel Drinkwater, aide-de-camp on Sir Gilbert Elliot's staff, was
much impressed by the fact that the Commodore
invited his guests to dine while the Spaniards were
overhauling them. Drinkwater was in the act of con-
gratulating Hardy on his release when the cry of
" man overboard " penetrated to the pleasant party.
The officers of the frigate sped to the quarter-deck,
and presently the Colonel beheld the large lieutenant,
who had so recently been by his side, in charge of a
jolly-boat being lowered into tumultuous waters.
" No sign of the missing man " was signalled, after an
anxious interval, but meanwhile the strong current of
the Straits was carrying the little boat far astern of the
Minerve. " By God! " exclaimed Commodore Nelson,
" I'll not lose Hardy! Back the mizzen-topsail."
That the Spaniards shortened sail, and the British
frigate recovered the jolly-boat seemed a miracle to
the landsmen, who had given themselves up for lost.
The explanation seemed to be that the enemy had
misinterpreted Nelson's extraordinary manœuvre, and
supposed that he had sighted the British Fleet approaching from the west to support him.

Fog enveloped the Straits that February night.

Colonel Drinkwater, too excited to sleep, was dimly conscious of strange sea-sounds, strange sails, very close. Nelson, who had given up his cabin to his guests, came in twice, and on the second occasion mentioned briefly that they were either amongst the Spanish Fleet or a convoy bound for the Antilles. Next morning it appeared that his first guess had been correct, but fog had been their friend.

The *Minerve* joined the Fleet, and Nelson moved back into the *Captain*. During the eve of St. Valentine's Day, 1797, the wind shifted to the westward, and Spanish signal guns sounded repeatedly.

Sir John Jervis detained the *Lively* frigate, which was to take Sir Gilbert Elliot home, to carry also the news of a Fleet action.

IV

Admiral Córdoba's orders were to put in at Cadiz, on his way to form a junction with the French Fleet at Brest. He had been blown far out into the Atlantic. Dawn on the grey morning of February 14th found him running, with the wind astern, twenty-five miles west of the Portuguese headland of St. Vincent, a hundred and fifty miles north-west of Cadiz. At 10.49 a.m., as dense mist began to clear, an historic conversation took place between the British Admiral and the First Captain of H.M.S. *Victory.*

"There are eight sail-of-the-line, Sir John."

" Very well, sir."

" There are twenty sail-of-the-line, Sir John . . .
Twenty-five . . . There are twenty-seven sail-of-the-
line, Sir John; near double our own . . ."

" Enough of that, sir! If there are fifty sail, I will
go through them. England badly needs a victory
at present."

The fine Spanish ships, described by the Signal
Lieutenant of the *Barfleur* as " thumpers, looking like
Beachy Head in a fog," were all undermanned, and
not in good order. Jervis quickly perceived that they
were proceeding leisurely, in a long straggling line,
and a gap of some seven miles stretched between their
leading division of six and the remaining one-and-
twenty. He sailed into the gap, with his fifteen ships,
due south in line ahead, and cut through without
much difficulty. The leading Spaniards sheered off
northwards, in an attempt to come round behind the
British; those in the van took a southerly course.
Jervis, who intended to deal with them first, hoisted
the signal to tack in succession. The Spanish backbone
was broken as, one by one, the British ships turned
north; but the possibility remained that the larger
Spanish division, by bearing up to pass astern, might
rejoin the smaller and perhaps escape to Cadiz.

It was at this moment that there occurred one of
the most famous episodes of sailing-ship warfare.
A British seventy-four wore out of the line, without
orders. Nelson, third from the rear, had appreciated

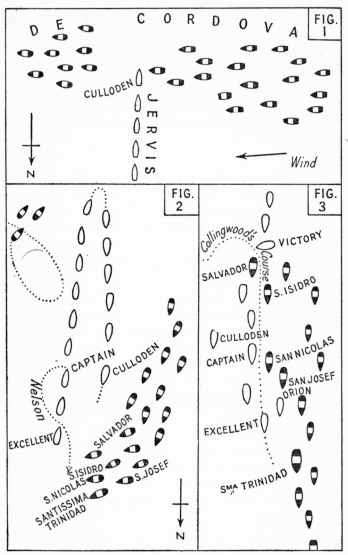

THE BATTLE OF CAPE ST. VINCENT

that the leading British ship might arrive too late to keep the gap open. He made a sweep to the east, and the *Captain* engaged seven Spaniards, three of them of over one hundred guns each. The *Santissima Trinidad*, reputed the largest warship in the world, was his first prey. A new friend (collected in Corsica), came to his assistance. " I was immediately joined, and most nobly supported, by the *Culloden*, Captain Troubridge . . . For near an hour, I believe (but do not pretend to be correct as to time) did the *Culloden* and *Captain* support this apparently, but not really, unequal contest; when the *Blenheim*, passing between us and the enemy, gave us a respite, and sickened the Dons." Jervis, having recognised the brilliance of Nelson's action, signalled the *Excellent* to support him. This ship was commanded by Collingwood, the foremost gunnery expert of his day, and a friend of Nelson since they had been lieutenants in Sir Peter Parker's Fleet. The trio held on to the enemy until other British ships came up, and the *mêlée* became general.

Nelson's second opportunity to make history came when Collingwood, firing into the 86-gun *San Nicolas* in a masterly manner, caused her to luff so that the great three-decker *San Josef* (already attacked by the *Prince George*) fell foul of her. The *Captain* had been so much mauled that she could be of no more service, in the line or in chase. Nelson ordered her helm to be put down, and called for a boarding party. He passed from the fore-chains of his own ship into the quarter galley of the *San Nicolas*, and a marine's musket

smashed an upper window for his entry into a Great
Cabin where all doors were locked. Some Spanish
officers discharged pistols through the skylights, while
the doors were being forced. Don Tomaso Geraldino
fell mortally wounded, on his own quarter-deck, but
the ceremony of several officers delivering their swords
to Nelson was interrupted by fire from the Admiral's
stern gallery of the *San Josef* which killed seven men
of the boarding party. This much larger ship was
inextricably entangled aloft with his first prize. He
determined to carry a Spanish first-rate from the
decks of a Spanish 80. He led his depleted party on,
to the cry of "Westminster Abbey, or Glorious
Victory." Fortunately, the appearance of resistance
from the *San Josef* was deceptive. As he came in sight,
a Spanish officer hailed to say that she surrendered,
and presently her Flag-Captain, on bended knee, presented his sword and explained that his Admiral was
dying of his wounds below. Nelson gave the fallen
enemy his hand and asked him to summon his officers
and ship's company to hear an announcement of the
surrender. So, "on the quarter-deck of a Spanish
first-rate, extravagant as the story may seem, did I
receive the swords of the vanquished Spaniards, which,
as I received, I gave to William Fearney, one of my
bargemen, who put them, with the greatest *sang-froid*,
under his arm."

He felt as if he was "in a dream" a few moments
later, when the *Victory* passed the interlocked group,
and her men, lining her bulwarks, saluted the *Captain*

with three cheers, an example followed by every ship in the British Fleet that evening when they distinguished the broad pendant of Commodore Nelson.

Darkness was falling as he went on board the *Victory* in considerable doubt how Jervis might receive him. But the Admiral had won his essential victory, and had decided to rest content with the possession of four enemy sail-of-the-line, and a light casualty list. He welcomed Nelson with open arms, " said he could not sufficiently thank me, and used every expression to make me happy." The scene was highly dramatic. Most of Nelson's hat had been shot away, his shirt and coat were in ribbons, and his countenance was blackened by gunpowder. His name appeared in the *Gazette* as " bruised but not obliged to quit the deck," but he had in fact received a superficial wound from a shell splinter, and his " contusion of no consequence" caused him acute pain for a week.

England, which had been badly needing a victory, received the news of the greatest naval battle since the Saints with acclamation. It was said that the King himself had chosen the title for Jervis—Earl of St. Vincent. After the victories of Rodney and Howe in 1782 and 1794, baronetcies had been given to their junior flag-officers. Nelson, to his relief, found himself Rear-Admiral Sir Horatio Nelson, K.B. He had no hope of issue, and was already having difficulty to " make ends meet." The Order of the Bath suited him much better than an hereditary title, and on taking flag rank, to which he had actually been promoted twelve days before the battle, in the ordinary course of seniority, he must relinquish his pay as a Colonel of Marines. To a curt account of his actions on " the most glorious Valentine's Day," he added a note. " There is a saying in the Fleet too flattering for me to omit telling—viz. ' Nelson's Patent Bridge for boarding First-Rates,' alluding to my passing over an Enemy's 80-gun ship." He chose as his supporters on his coat-of-arms a sailor and a British lion, and for his crest the stern of a Spanish Man-of-War, proper, inscribed " San Josef."

* 3 *

Santa Cruz, Teneriffe

LADY NELSON wrote typically to her husband after the battle of Cape St. Vincent:

"Thank God you are well, and Josiah. My anxiety was far beyond my powers of expression. M. Nelson and Captain Locker behaved humanely and attentive to me. They wrote immediate, Captain Locker assuring me that you were perfectly well, Maurice urging me not to believe idle reports, the *Gazette* saying you were slightly wounded . . . Altogether, my dearest husband, my sufferings were great . . . I shall not be myself till I hear from you again. What can I attempt to say to you about boarding? You have been most wonderfully Protected; you have done desperate actions enough. Now may I—indeed I do—beg that you never board again: LEAVE IT for CAPTAINS."

When she had heard his own account of his exploits, she repeated her injunctions, "that all these wonderful and desperate actions—such as boarding Ships—you will leave to others." She told him that everyone was

L.N. 49 **D**

agreed that his character could not stand higher, " therefore rest satisfied." Unfortunately, the only result of such tender messages was that she lost influence. They found Nelson in charge of the inshore squadron off Cadiz, and in the *Sketch of My Life* supplied by him to the editor of his biography for the *Naval Chronicle* two years later, he mentioned: " It was during this period that perhaps my personal courage was more conspicuous than at any other period of my life." Detractors, as he rose to fame (and critics ever after), were to deplore that Nelson was vain. It was pointed out that he rejoiced in decorations and orders; he could be theatrical. But this often-quoted sentence scribbled in a hurry, and perfectly correct in fact, stands unique in the vast mass of material that flowed from his pen during his forty-seven years. It was natural to him to be theatrical, and the life of a sailor, especially in time of war, is dramatic, say what he will.

The Spanish Fleet was in port, still strong in numbers, and it was at first supposed that they might make a dash for Ferrol. By the beginning of July, Nelson was attempting to force them out, by throwing shell amongst them, and into the town. In a sharp skirmish with enemy gunboats, he nearly lost his life. " This was a service, hand-to-hand, with swords." His barge, with a crew of ten, a coxswain, Fremantle and himself, was attacked by that of the Spanish Commander, pulled by two dozen men and carrying four officers. Fremantle got a slight wound, but John Sykes, coxswain, who twice interposed his person when Nelson was about to be cut down, was in hospital for weeks.

St. Vincent had good reason for ordering these nightly diversions. At home the mutiny at Spithead had been followed by the mutiny at the Nore, and ships which had been affected were being sent out to a Chief with a name for severity. (" What do they mean by invariably sending me the mutinous ships? Do they think I will be hangman to the Fleet? ") The *Theseus* (74), into which Nelson had changed in May, had come to him with the curse of a bad reputation. St. Vincent, after stating that she was " an abomination," blandly added that her condition, the result of a futile Captain and a bullying First Lieutenant, would soon be put to rights by Admiral Nelson and Captain Miller. Nelson found her absolutely destitute of stores, and set to work with characteristic energy to discover whether he had got with her a set of scoundrels or " the stuff to work upon."

A stiffening of " old Agamemnons " were soon teaching their new companions how to construct siege ladders, which filled them with interest, and curiosity as to where they were to be used. It gradually became known to them that when Spanish market boatmen failed to deliver sufficient greens for his people, Admiral Nelson interviewed the unsatisfactory vendors personally. He had gone to the *Swiftsure*, where two fellows, accused of shamming mad in order to get their discharge, were lying in irons, after attempts to destroy themselves. After inspecting them, he had written to the Commander-in-Chief asking that Dr. Weir, Physician to the Fleet, should report upon them. He had then offered to give fifty pounds out of his own pocket to send one of the men to a proper place for his recovery, and recommended both for discharge. Within a fortnight of his move into the *Theseus* a scrap of paper signed in tipsy capitals " SHIP'S COMPANY " was brought to him. It had been found during the middle watch, dropped on the quarter-deck:

> " Success attend Admiral Nelson! God bless Captain Miller! We thank them for the Officers they have placed over us. We are happy and comfortable, and will shed every drop of blood in our veins, and the name of the *Theseus* shall be immortalized as high as the *Captain's*."

But the expedition upon which he sailed, in command of four of the line, three frigates, and the *Fox* cutter, early on the morning of Saturday, July 15th, was not to be a success.

II

St. Vincent had failed to persuade the Generals at Gibraltar to part with troops " to attempt the surprise of Santa Cruz in the Grand Canary," and by the time that he agreed to Nelson's suggestions, he knew that the Mexican treasure fleet, having received news of the British victory on Valentine's Day, had not put into that port. It appeared certain, however, that two register ships bound from Manila for Cadiz, were there, and had not yet unloaded their rich cargoes. Nelson affirmed that if he was given two hundred extra marines, " with General Troubridge ashore, and myself afloat, I am confident of success," and St. Vincent, after considerable hesitation, pronounced himself ready " to dash you off." He could not hope to return to the Mediterranean at present, and he was being worried by courts martial. (" I dread not the seamen. It is the indiscreet, licentious conversation of the officers which produce all our ills, and the presumptuous discussion of the orders they receive.") He empowered a " lucky" commander to chose the ships and officers to accompany him, and made no objection when Nelson's choice represented the cream of the late Mediterranean Fleet: Troubridge, Fremantle, Miller, Waller, Bowen and the young Sam Hood.

Troubridge, who had recently concluded a lightning wooing of Miss Betsy Wynne, took his bride with him. Their wedding had been staged by Lady Hamilton at the British Embassy, Naples, and Mrs. Troubridge was enchanted at the prospect of seeing service in H.M.S. *Inconstant*. " We are going," she wrote jubilantly in her diary, " to take the island of Teneriffe."

Towards sunset, after a prosperous passage of five days, a blue cone, girded by drifting cloud, became visible. This was the famous Peak. The last conference for Captains was held on board the *Theseus* and Troubridge was entrusted by his Admiral with the summons to the Governor or Commanding Officer of Santa Cruz to be presented, as he found best, either before or after proceeding against the town and mole-head battery. All available men were transferred to the frigates, and Nelson, with his line-of-battle ships, retired to the eastward, to wear and tack throughout a night which was undisturbed by any warlike sounds. With dawn it became apparent that the surprise attack under cover of dark had failed. Owing to the conjunction of a strong gale in the offing and an unexpected current against them in-shore, the landing parties had not been able to get within a mile of the beach chosen for their disembarkation. A further attempt was made in broad daylight from the land side but, owing to a flat calm and contrary currents, the 74s ordered to engage the batteries could not even reach anchoring ground.

By Monday morning, July 24th, Nelson had decided upon a night attack direct on the town, led by him in person. The enemy were now well prepared, but he was " confident in the bravery of those who would be employed." By 5.30 p.m. the squadron was at anchor two miles north of an antique town, in the Spanish style, backed by volcanic heights, and as a wild wet night closed in the Admiral concluded his arrangements by burning Lady Nelson's letters. Her son came in while he was so engaged, and his accoutrements proclaimed that, although Officer of the Watch, he intended to embark with the landing-party. The first dramatic dialogue of a fatal night took place:

" Should we both fall, Josiah, what would become of your poor mother? The care of the *Theseus* falls to you. Stay, therefore, and take charge of her."

" Sir, the Ship must take care of herself. I will go with you to-night if never again."

Before setting out upon what he frankly considered a " forlorn hope . . . I never expected to return," Nelson, attended by Bowen, Miller and Hood, supped with Mrs. Fremantle in the *Seahorse* frigate. The bride gathered that " the taking of the place seemed an easy, almost a sure thing," and although the noise made by the men of the *Theseus* as they went on board the boats bound for the mole was vexing, she retired, after the last of her guests had gone over the side into black darkness, quite at ease in her mind. When they heard much firing during the next few hours, she and her companions had no doubt that Nelson was now master of Teneriffe. " Great was our mistake. This proved to be a shocking unfortunate night"

Nelson received his wound, a musket ball shattering the right elbow, either as he was stepping out of a boat on to the mole of Santa Cruz, under heavy fire, or just after he had landed. Lieutenant Nisbet, missing him, returned in search, and applied a tourniquet. This was the great hour of one of the most unsatisfactory of stepsons for, after he had collected a crew of five, and got a grounded boat afloat, Nisbet himself took an oar, and shouted to the steersman to go as close as possible under the guns of the mole battery,

which were in action. Nelson recovered consciousness,
and asked to be lifted, at the moment that the *Fox*
cutter, struck in her magazine by a 24-pound shot,
went down, taking with her her Commander and
ninety-seven men. The Admiral insisted that his boat
should go out of her course to pick up survivors, and
presently refused to approach the *Seahorse*, although
strongly advised that further exposure might cost him
his life. " Then I will die; for I would rather suffer
death than alarm Mrs. Fremantle by her seeing me in
this state when I can give her no tidings whatever of
her husband."

When they got within hail of the *Theseus*, he rejected
the offer of a chair from the main yardarm, to hoist
him in, and he pulled himself up the ship's side,
shouting, " with a spirit that astonished all," orders
for the boat to return at once to the spot where men
of the *Fox* were still struggling in the surf, and for the
surgeon to get his instruments ready. " For I know
that I must lose my arm, and the sooner it is off, the
better."

The amputation, " very high, near the shoulder,"
was performed forthwith by Mr. Thomas Eshelby,
Principal Medical Officer, assisted by a First Mate,
M. Louis Remonier, a French Royalist refugee,
collected by Hood's Fleet at Toulon. During it, the
enemy began a bombardment of the English shipping
in the bay, and the *Theseus*, standing off and on the
town, returned fire regularly. With dawn, a boat
which had managed to escape from a scene of disaster,

brought in the news that the three hundred men of
the landing-parties who had managed to struggle
ashore to the appointed rendezvous had surrendered
to a force of eight thousand. Troubridge had sent in
a flag of truce. He had no alternative. Most of the
boats had missed the mole altogether, and had been
stove in the surf. The scaling ladders had been lost,
and the powder soaked.

The Commandant of the Canaries, who could well
afford it, behaved with generosity. Within two days
all survivors had been returned to their ships, and the
squadron, provisioned from the town, was at liberty
to depart in peace. Nelson, not to be outdone in
courtesy, offered to carry the Commandant's despatches
to Cadiz, " thus making himself the herald of his
own defeat."

He had stood the operation well. Eshelby reported
him " quite easy," but wisely prescribed nothing
more than tea, soup, sago, lemonade and tamarind
drinks for a difficult patient whose temperature was
rising. In a dictated despatch to St. Vincent, Nelson
appended his second left-hand signature. He had
already sent little Mrs. Fremantle a line. But his
spirits sank as he detailed two hundred and fifty-odd
officers, seamen, and marines, killed, wounded or
missing, and to add to his dejection the wind refused
to carry his ships out of sight of shores which all now
detested. Tom Allen, in preparation for a blowing
passage, had rigged up a string, attached to his shirt
collar, which Sir Horatio, if restless, need only twitch

to summon his body-servant, but day after day the *Theseus* lay becalmed. It was not until the afternoon of August 16th that the squadron joined the Fleet and Nelson addressed himself once more to his Chief.

"MY DEAR SIR,

"I rejoice at being once more in sight of your flag, and with your permission will come on board the *Ville de Paris* and pay you my respects. If the *Emerald* has joined, you know my wishes. A left-handed Admiral will never again be considered useful therefore the sooner I get to a very humble cottage the better, and make room for a better man to serve the State.

"But whatever my lot, believe me with the most sincere affection ever your most faithful

HORATIO NELSON "

His handwriting in youth had been a conventional " fine Italian." That had long degenerated into a thin sloping scribble. His new script was square, upright, but tending to topple backwards, and at present very tremulous. It was nevertheless, particularly legible, and a specimen of Nelson's " left-hand write " whenever it is displayed, in sale room or museum, is at once recognisable.

St. Vincent's reply was handsome. " Mortals cannot command success." He had no doubt that Nelson and his companions had deserved both success and fame. The *Seahorse* should waft him and Fremantle home without delay. He sent his love to Mrs. Fremantle, and hoped to salute her and make his bow to Nelson's stump to-morrow morning. The result of this was that he got Nelson to dine the same evening. A man who feared himself " a burthen to my friends and useless to my Country," was very anxious to represent himself as ready for further employment afloat. St. Vincent promised him privately that he would ask for him as soon as possible, and wrote home, " I have very good ground of hope he will be restored to the service of his King and Country."

Admiral Nelson came on board the *Seahorse* in great spirits, but Mrs. Fremantle, who had not seen him since his operation, found " it looks shocking to be without one arm." She confided her own symptoms to his Principal Medical Officer, and Mr. Eshelby thought that the Captain of the *Seahorse* should find himself a father next March.

Meanwhile, a very trying passage had to be endured by a company of invalids. Fremantle, whose flesh wound was causing him great pain, was beginning to fear that he too would soon have to face amputation. Nelson wryly confessed himself " very indifferent." But when they anchored at Spithead, although the weather was much too rough for a lady to leave the ship, a one-armed Admiral descended to his barge without delay.

He surprised his family by a sudden arrival at Bath on the night of September 3rd. His wife, sitting with his father, his sister, Mrs. Bolton, and a niece, " little Kate," recognised a peremptory voice shouting orders

to the driver of a post-chaise. A moment later Nelson
was, as he had always promised, " come laughing
back." Four years had passed since his family had
seen him, and the fixed, dim right eye and empty
sleeve were painful novelties. He appeared to have
retained his old infective high spirits, but a doctor had
to be summoned at once to replace a dressing put on
at dawn, at Portsmouth; and a Bath physician
acceded smoothly to the Admiral's suggestion of a
London opinion.

III

Sir Horatio and Lady Nelson arrived at 141 Bond
Street, and he delivered himself into the hands of
London experts. He looked upon his condition as the
result of an accident, not an illness, and went down
to the Admiralty most mornings; but he took a firm
line when he was notified that 6 p.m. at Surgeon's
Hall had been appointed for an examination of his
claim for a pension for the loss of an eye in 1794.
London was fog-bound; he had no carriage, and
Surgeon's Hall was in the City. He offered to present
himself during hours of daylight and did so in jocund
mood. (" Oh! this is only for an eye: in a few days
I shall come for an arm: and in a little time longer,
God knows, most probably for a leg.") His wife's
bulletins disclosed that he was in " a good deal of
pain." " Opium procures him rest." Some nights he
was " pretty quiet." He pronounced " my domestic

happiness perfect," but it was always the fate of a most unlucky woman to bear him company when he was down on his luck. During his dreadful five years of unemployment, on half pay, the wolf had never been absent from the door. He was back on half pay now, on a much more exalted scale, it was true, but the Bond Street lodgings were very expensive, and poor value. When brother officers began to call, as they soon did, in large numbers, Lady Nelson could only offer what she deprecatingly described as " a family dinner." However, it appeared to her that some of her guests were very rough diamonds.

The Nelsons, accompanied by Sir Gilbert Elliot, who was about to become Lord Minto, shared an equipage down to Greenwich, to visit Captain Locker; and in the stately residence of the Lieutenant Governor, the Admiral gave sittings, at the request of his old Captain, to Mr. Lemuel Abbott. The date was an unfortunate one for a flattering likeness, but the result was the prototype of the portrait to be recognised by succeeding generations as Nelson. Abbot repeated it, again and again, with a hat and without, and added decorations, as years passed. Travesties were to swing in the breeze outside innumerable licensed premises.

The press noticed the event when Admiral Nelson was invested with the Order of the Bath at St. James's Palace at the first levée of the winter season. He had presented two gentlemen—the Rev. William Nelson (who was living in hopes of a stall at Norwich) and his late Flag Captain. " You have lost your right arm!" exclaimed George III, pausing and peering as he came to a junior Admiral whom he failed to recognise. "But not my right hand, sir, as I have the honour of presenting Captain Berry." Afterwards royalty returned to say in the kindliest manner to a man who said he was well and looked so ill, "But your Country has a claim for a bit more of you."

On October 13th the Park and Tower guns fired in honour of Admiral Duncan's victory over the Dutch Fleet at Camperdown; official illuminations were ordered and most private houses attempted some decoration. A party of patriots in liquor banged on the doors of 141 Bond Street, where every window was black. It happened that nobody in the house had heard either the guns or the news. The invalid, after a bad day, had taken a sleep-inducing draught. When the intruders learned that Admiral Nelson, severely wounded at Teneriffe, lodged here they withdrew in hot apology. "You will hear no more from us to-night." But the mere thought of a decisive engagement between the North Sea Fleet and the Dutch had been troubling Nelson for days past. ("I would give this other arm to be with Duncan at this moment!") For it was now three months since the ligature of silk (French fashion) had been applied by M. Remonier on board H.M.S. *Theseus*, and the stump was becoming fiery and swollen. The advisability of a further operation had been discussed, and he was ready, but the doctors disagreed. He was soothingly advised that the cure must be left to time and Nature.

He dragged himself down to his native Norfolk, to be enrolled a Freeman of Norwich amongst much festivity, and seized the occasion to look for what he had always needed—a home of his own. Roundwood Farm, two miles from Ipswich, was inspected and bought, somewhat to the dismay of Lady Nelson, who had long been inured to living in her boxes, and preferred lodgings in fashionable spas, or the metropolis. On their return to London, Nelson heard that he was to be given H.M.S. *Foudroyant* (86), due to be launched in January and commissioned in February. Lord Spencer also warned him that His Majesty's going to St. Paul's to return thanks for the naval victories of the war was fixed for December 19th. This meant many a long hour jolting in a carriage with other flag-officers in full-dress uniform, but Nelson enjoyed ceremonies so long as he was not the chief speaker. Gloom settled upon him at the prospect of addressing a large blandishing civilian audience, and he departed to receive a gold box of the value of one hundred guineas at the Guildhall on November 28th, doggedly reminding himself, " Anything better than ingratitude."

Five nights later, when London was lying hushed in a snow-scene, he slept the night through without recourse to drugs and woke calm as a child. When the surgeon (fetched in haste) undid the bandages, the ligature which had held fast to the artery and nerve so long, attended by such loathsome odours, came away at the slightest touch. Within a few days the stump was healing. The *Foudroyant* would not be ready for him in time.

On the night of December 8th he wrote two notes. The first, to Captain Berry, R.N., was headed SECRET. " If you mean to marry, I would recommend your doing it speedily, or the to-be Mrs. Berry will have very little of your company; for I am well, and you may expect to be called for every hour. . . ." The second was addressed to the clergyman of the nearest parish church, St. George's, Hanover Square. " An officer desires to return thanks to Almighty God for his perfect recovery from a severe Wound, and also for many mercies bestowed upon him. December 8th, 1787 (for next Sunday)."

* 4 *
The Nile

D URING THE early months of 1798, while General Buonaparte, summoned from Italy, was inspecting the invasion ports of the north coast of France, all Europe was waiting fascinated to see which country the revolutionary crocodile would devour next. Austria, complaining that her Italian campaign had been wrecked by the withdrawal of the British Fleet from the Mediterranean, had relinquished Belgium, in exchange for the city and part of the territories of Venetia. Holland, Switzerland and the Italian Republics were all occupied by French troops. Lord Malmesbury's efforts to conclude a peace, at Lille, had been frustrated. The Anglophile Catherine of Russia had died, suddenly, and France had no fears of her successor. In February, Buonaparte, who thought poorly of the preparations for the invasion of England, sent the Directory two alternative suggestions. The first was for a descent on the north-west German coast with the object of cutting off Britain's commerce with central Europe. The second, which had been his favourite since November, was for an expedition on a large scale to the Orient. His conquests in Italy had placed great naval resources at the disposal of France. Venetia, Genoa, Spezia, Leghorn, Civita Vecchia and Ancona were all ready to supply warships, transports, stores and sailors. The conquest of Egypt was agreed upon. But excellent secrecy was maintained as to the destination of the armada fitting out at many southern French and Italian ports to augment the main Fleet at Toulon. Ireland, the West Indies, Naples, Sicily and Portugal were all mentioned in the English Press as possibilities. At Whitehall it was realised that at all costs the junction of this armament with the Brest squadron, or the Spanish Fleet still held in Cadiz, must be prevented. On April 30th, Lord Spencer wrote to Lord St. Vincent urging that " the appearance of a British squadron in the Mediterranean is a condition on which the fate of Europe may at this moment be stated to depend." Nelson joined St. Vincent, off Cadiz, in time to dine, that day.

Afterwards, a number of persons plumed themselves on having recommended that so junior an officer should be given a detached command in the Mediterranean. Lord Minto remembered a call upon Lord Spencer with the express object of mentioning the very unusual qualifications of Sir Horatio. The First Lord claimed that he had already made up his mind. Actually, the nomination lay with St. Vincent. Finally, Prince William Henry, in confidence, empowered Edward Berry to tell Nelson that as a matter of fact His Majesty himself had chosen him.

Two days after he had reported to St. Vincent, Nelson was sent off, up the Mediterranean in H.M.S. *Vanguard* with a small squadron. He had long been " panting to be in actual service." This was his first cruise since his loss of an arm. A fortnight at sea had set him up. His agonising months of protracted invalidism were pushed out of his mind, and he was in ebullient spirits, " exhilarated beyond description," when a violent northerly gale blew him off the Sicilian coast, partially dismasted the *Vanguard*, and dispersed his squadron. His flagship was refitted, and jury masts were rigged, in record time, and he sailed again, from S. Pietro in Sardinia, only to discover, off Toulon, that the French expedition had put to sea with the same wind which had proved so disastrous to him.

Near Cape Corse, on June 7th, he received new instructions. Troubridge, with ten of-the-line, and the *Leander* (50) had been sent to him, and his orders were to proceed in search of the French Fleet, to any part of the Mediterranean, the Adriatic, the Greek archipelago or even the Black Sea, and when he had found it, to take, burn or destroy it. These satisfying but large commands found him becalmed, with the knowledge that Buonaparte had already sailed, " with a long start," and " frigates, the Eyes of the Fleet," were not at his disposal. Since the night of the great storm he had never seen the four which had accompanied him from Cadiz. He knew that they were safe, but, deeming that a ship so severely damaged as the *Vanguard* must return to a dockyard, they had betaken themselves to Gibraltar. He wrote at once to Sir William Hamilton, asking for information and frigates from Naples, and he followed his letter by a personal envoy. " Troubridge will say everything I could put in a ream of paper."

Hardy, who had been sent in his despatch brig, the *Mutine*, to look into Telamon Bay, had joined him off the Ponza Islands with a report that there was no sign of Buonaparte there. A Tunisian cruiser had seen the French Fleet steering to the eastward, on June 4th. By the 15th, a startling theory had suggested itself to Nelson. " If they pass Sicily, I shall believe they are going on their scheme of possessing Alexandria—a plan concerted with Tippoo Saib, by no means so difficult as might at first be imagined."

Forty-eight hours after he had sent Troubridge in the *Mutine* to Naples, letters from the Palazzo Sessa were brought out to him. Lady Hamilton's first note merely expressed warm good wishes; her second contained an enclosure.

" Dear Sir, I send you a letter I have this moment received from the Queen. *Kiss it*, and send it back by Bowen, as I am bound not to give any of her letters, Ever yours, Emma."

He replied in haste, before sailing for the Straits of Messina, " I have kissed the Queen's letter." The news with which Troubridge had returned was not wholly satisfactory. Sir William Hamilton had evidently done his best. He had taken the two British sea-officers to General Acton, but etiquette had

demanded that the anti-British Secretary of State, the
Marquis de Gallo, should be present at the interview,
and de Gallo could not advise a King " perfectly
at peace with France " to supply frigates to Admiral
Nelson.   By the terms of the late treaty with the
Directory, not more than four belligerent ships at a
time might enter Neapolitan ports.   Acton had done
all he could in furnishing Troubridge with " a sort of
credential " asking all Port Governors to give the
English squadron every necessary assistance and
supply, " under the rose."   Nelson replied officially,
and very stiffly, pointing out that the French Minister
at Naples had been allowed to send off vessels to
Buonaparte describing the strength and destination of
the British squadron, lying at anchor, outside neutral
waters, but that no corresponding information had
been available for Troubridge.

A rumour that Malta had fallen was confirmed to
him off Cape Passaro, on June 22nd, but Buonaparte,
having taken the island bloodlessly, had left a
garrison there and sailed again the next day, it was
supposed for Sicily.   Since the response from Naples
had clearly shown that the King of the Two Sicilies
did not expect invasion, Nelson remained in his previous belief that Alexandria must be the enemy's goal.
He guessed that they might at present be in Corfu,
but without frigates, could only guess.   He sent Hardy
ahead with a despatch for the British Consul at
Alexandria (" Pray do not detain the *Mutine* for I
am in a fever at not finding the French ") and set

out on a six-days' passage for the chief port of Egypt.

At Alexandria he found no French Fleet and no news of it. The British Consul was on holiday in England, and his deputy was neither British nor helpful. The disappointment was terrible, and during his passage to Candia, Nelson composed a long despatch, explaining why he had been without news of the enemy for a month, which stately Captain Ball of H.M.S. *Alexander* strongly advised him not to send. But Nelson was under no delusions that his appointment was not being criticised, and was beginning to feel the strain of chasing a phantom enemy. " After receiving Captain Hardy's report, I stretched the Fleet over to the coast of Asia." He had looked up the Aleppo coast, and into the Turkish gulf of Antalya.

By July 20th he was at Syracuse for the second time, with ships some of which had not been watered since May 6th, and all of which, although provisioned for another nine or ten weeks, were deficient in anti-scorbutics. He afterwards said that the return to Syracuse had broken his heart, and that two days before he got there his spirits had reached their lowest ebb. His intention now, since he had evidently guessed wrong about Egypt, was to try the Morea, Constantinople, and after them Cyprus. Writing to Sir William Hamilton formally, from Syracuse, he sent bitter complaint that he had been refused entry (" I understood that private orders at least would have been given "); and to St. Vincent he mentioned his treatment as shameful. Lady Hamilton also received an indignant note. On the following day, July 22nd, his tune suddenly changed. He told Sir William, " The Fleet is unmoored, and the moment the wind comes off the land, shall go out of this delightful harbour, where our present wants have been most amply supplied and where every attention has been paid to us." He added something irreconcilable unless it was intended to shield those who had assisted him " under the rose "—a repetition of his previous regrets that no private orders had been sent to the Governor for his admission.

On the back of an order of no particular sig-nificance, of this date, in his Letter Book, which passed into the possession of Lady Hamilton after his death, the unhappy woman wrote wildly, " The Queen's Letter, privately got by me, got him and his Fleet victualled and watered in a few days." Her evidence was long suspect, for one of her principal claims for a pension for public services was that but for her agency the battle of the Nile could not have been fought. James Harrison, a dreadful hack summoned by her to produce a biography of Nelson which should give readers an idealistic picture of her influence over the hero, offered a perfect farrago about a " talismanic gift " given to her secretly by the Queen of Naples, some password or token, only to be used in direst need, so potent that at the sight of it any Sicilian Governor would become hypnotised and bound to silence " by the dread of an assured death." From the facts now available, it appears that Lady Hamilton did approach

the Queen, that the squadron was supplied, and that
Nelson, in his last codicil, attributed this to Lady
Hamilton's influence. More cannot be said, but there
seems no longer any reason to doubt the authenticity
of a typically Nelsonian letter printed by Harrison,
of which the original has not yet come to light:

" MY DEAR FRIENDS,
    " Thanks to your exertions, we have victualled and
    watered; and surely watering at the Fountains of
    Arethusa, we must have victory. We shall sail with
    the first breeze, and be assured I will return, either
    crowned with laurel, or covered with cypress."

After his departure from Syracuse, Nelson made the
Gulf of Coron, in the Morea, within the week, and
there learned that Buonaparte's armament had been
observed, steering to the south-east from Candia about
a month past. Gradually he came to realise that he
had missed the enemy twice, but by arriving too soon,
not too late. On the first occasion, soon after leaving
Syracuse, on June 22nd in thick weather, his proximity
had caused Admiral de Brueys to hasten his slow-
moving armada towards the security of Crete. On
June 29th, the British squadron had scarcely left
Alexandria when watchers from the Pharos had begun
to see French sails approaching from the north-
west.

Nelson's second passage to Alexandria occupied
four days, and during it he summoned his Captains
for conference whenever possible. It had always been

his hope to " fall in with the French at sea, to try Buonaparte on a wind," and the disposal and conduct of each ship under every likely combination of circumstances had been so often discussed that his intentions were perfectly familiar to every senior officer under his command. Not even Troubridge knew, as yet, that as day after day had passed without bringing the action for which he was always ready, Nelson had reached such a condition of nervous tension that the least unfamiliar sound sent his heart racing—a bad habit which, he said, was to persist for the rest of his life.

The squadron came in sight of the Pharos, with a top-gallant wind, in clear weather, soon after midday on August 1st, 1797. As before, neither the old port nor what they called the Frank's port showed a French sail. The signal to turn east, down the coast, was flung out, and in every ship dinner, usually served at 1.30, began. Saumarez of the *Orion* did not think he had ever felt more hopeless.

" Judge what a change took place when, as the cloth was being removed, the Officer of the Watch came running in saying ' Sir, a signal is just now made that the Enemy is in Aboukir Bay and moored in a line of Battle.' "

II

By a happy chance, the outstanding features of the greatest victory that had graced the British Navy since the days of the Armada were all highly dramatic, and easily to be understood by the general public.

Admiral de Brueys, anchored in a crescent-shaped formation on the edge of shoal water, with the fortified isle of Aboukir to the windward end of his line, had rightly supposed that the English would lack charts of the reefs protecting his position. When he was informed that British ships were approaching the bay, he concluded that they would not attempt a night action. He called a council of war, at which only one of his officers advised that he should order his fleet to weigh and stand out to meet the enemy, who were continuing to bear up for the bay, now with a whole-sail breeze. About 5.30 he signalled that he intended to engage them at anchor. His frigates had not been on the look-out, and boats of many of his ships-of-the-line, with working parties, were on shore. He expected the attack from the seaward side, and in their hurry and confusion (as the British were observed to be coming to the wind in succession) not only did the French fail to cast their larboard guns loose, they piled up amongst them mess furniture and baggage. De Brueys had placed his strongest ships, including his own flagship, *L'Orient* (120), in the centre of the line, and his next heaviest in the only other position he supposed vulnerable, his rear. His fleet consisted of thirteen of-the-line (three of them 80s) and four large frigates. Nelson was bearing down upon him with ten 74s, one 50 and the little *Mutine*. Of the remaining three British 74s, two were detached on scouting duty

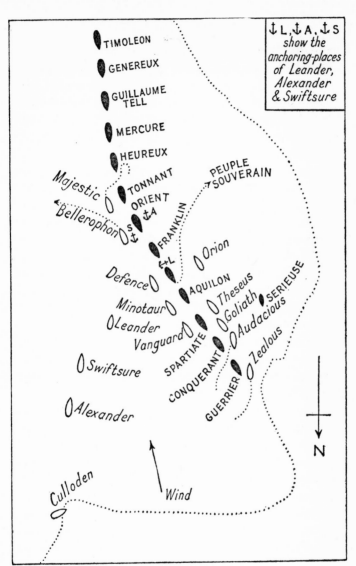

THE BATTLE OF THE NILE

and the third was nine miles astern, with an enemy wine-brig in tow.

Nelson gave the signal to attack the enemy van, which contained de Brueys' oldest and least effective craft, for he had instantly noted that the leading ship was not so close to the island as to prevent an entry, and that there was also room for ships to pass through the French line and attack the centre. ("Where there was room for a French 74 at single anchor to swing, there was room for a British 74 to anchor.") The problem of attacking a stationary enemy after dark had long been discussed by him with his Captains. After he had ordered his squadron to form line of battle, and get ready to anchor by the stern, no further signal was necessary. The risks of entering a strange bay at sunset and without charts or pilots, were great, but only the *Culloden* (Troubridge) struck the tail of the shoal and was reduced throughout the action to serving as a beacon to vessels coming up astern. The *Vanguard*, the sixth ship in the line, was the first to anchor outside.

By 6.28, when the brief tropical twilight was fast fading, the five leading British ships were all inside the French line, and bringing to bear upon the enemy van, at close range, a tremendous and overwhelming fire. Half an hour later, a scene of destruction was lit by nothing but gunfire. Five French 74s, undermanned and able to fight only one broadside at a time, were being swiftly pounded into helplessness by eight British; de Brueys' six remaining ships, out of the fight to leeward, awaited their fate in despair. The eighth and ninth of Nelson's ships, hastening to a smoke-hung quarter, sustained the heaviest casualties. The *Bellerophon* brought up abreast of *L'Orient*, twice her size, and the *Majestic* ran her jib-boom into the main rigging of *L'Heureux* and suffered the loss of her Captain before she was freed to begin an unsupported action with *Le Tonnant*.

About 8 p.m. Nelson, standing on his quarter-deck (according to tradition looking at a sketch of the Bay taken out of a French prize, a few days previously), was struck on the head by a piece of scrap shot. His brow was cut to the bone, above his old Calvi wound, and he fell, blinded, with the words, " I am killed. Remember me to my wife." But his " bright " eye had merely been obscured by a flap of flesh, and profuse hæmorrhage, and when the wound had been stitched and bandaged, he demanded to be assisted on deck again. In the cockpit he had refused to allow the Principal Surgeon to be told that the Admiral was amongst the wounded, and in the bread-room, to which he had withdrawn to clear the cock-pit, he had pushed up his bandages and begun to trace the opening words of a despatch. " My Lord, Almighty God has blessed His Majesty's Arms in the late Battle . . ."

He emerged into the dark-blue Egyptian night just in time to witness an incident which became the subject of many paintings and engravings—*L'Orient* taking with her to the depths of Aboukir Bay the body of de Brueys, dead of his wounds, the gold and diamonds

collected by Buonaparte from Switzerland and Rome
to finance the Eastern Expedition upon which he had
departed inland, and the treasures of the Hospital of
St. John of Jerusalem, removed after the seizure of
Malta. The explosion on board the enemy flagship
shocked watchers in Rosetta ten miles distant. In
H.M.S. *Alexander* Captain Ball carefully preserved to
send to his Chief an object which had descended from
the air undamaged upon his quarter-deck—one of
the silver forks used at the table of de Brueys. Nelson's
officers, in the intervals of garnering the spoils of
victory, in extremely hot weather, hilariously founded
the Crocodile Club. They sent to Sir Horatio an
invitation to accept the gift of a sword and have his
portrait taken for the Society. Their own features
were to become familiar to many British homes, for
to have been a Captain at the Battle of the Nile was
to have become a hero.

III

Nelson's despatches, announcing an action which he
pardonably styled a conquest, took two months to
reach London, and the days while he lay, pain-
stricken, and with a high temperature, in his cot in
Aboukir roads, were amongst the strangest in his
history. He had come to the end of more than a
chapter in his life, but for lack of frigates he could not,
immediately, tell the world what had happened. He
had achieved a victory so decisive that Europe was to

ring with his name. Every circumstance connected
with it was calculated to touch the fancy, particularly
of a sea-faring nation. He was young and modest.
He had omitted to enter his own name in the casualty
list; he had given all the credit to his officers. (" My
band of friends was irresistible.") He had sent to the
City of London a French Admiral's sword " as a
remembrance that Britannia still rules the waves."
A peerage, a succession of honours and rewards were
to be showered upon him, but as yet all he realised
was that his head was splitting, and that " had it
pleased God that I had not been wounded and stone
blind, there cannot be a doubt but that every ship
would have been in our possession." Only two of-the-
line and two frigates had escaped him, but he had
hoped for annihilation.

In London, as weeks had passed with no news,
anxiety had been great. Mr. Pitt and Lord Spencer
had been patient; old Admiral Goodall, when asked,
" What is your favourite Hero about? " had grunted,
" I know him. Something capital." Mr. Dundas
had presumed that when Sir Horatio reappeared he
would be able to produce at least a good reason for
having missed Buonaparte. Lord Grenville had been
insistent that he ought to be ordered to protect the
Kingdom of the Two Sicilies, and abandon a vain
chase of the French Fleet. Relief, when the truth, so
much exceeding the most optimistic expectation,
became known, was commensurate. When the First
Lord read that the victory had not entailed the loss

of a single British ship, he fainted away. At Naples, both the Queen and Lady Hamilton had swooned, but the Ambassadress had, with typical resilience, rallied to drive about the streets in an open carriage with two midshipmen, wearing around her brows a bandeau inscribed " Nelson and Victory."

Nelson himself, urged by both the Hamiltons to " come soon," approached Naples with reluctance. His hopes for the immediate future were for leave to go home, and that the command should devolve upon Troubridge. His progress towards a scene of un-bridled festivity was slow. The *Vanguard* had lost her foremast, the head of her main-topmast and her jib-boom, in a squall on the night of September 15th. A week later the wounded flagship of the Saviour of Europe entered Naples bay in tow of a frigate. Sir William Hamilton's barge, accompanied by a boat-load of musicians who had learnt " Rule Britannia " and " See the Conquering Hero," was the first of the five hundred-odd craft thronging glassy waters, to come alongside the Admiral. Nelson's own account of what followed was sent to his wife from the British Embassy a few days later.

" Alongside came my honoured friends: the scene in the boat was terribly affecting; up flew her ladyship, and exclaiming: ' Oh God is it possible? ' she fell into my arms more dead than alive. Tears, however soon set matters to rights. . . . I hope some day to have the pleasure of intro-

Plate 1 Lady Nelson. Miniature by Daniel Orme

Plate 2 Lady Hamilton as a bacchante. Miniature by Henry Bone

ducing you to Lady Hamilton, she is one of the best women in this world. How few could have made the turn she has. She is an honour to her sex, and a proof that a reputation may be regained. I own, it requires a great soul. . . . May God Almighty bless you, and give us, in due time, a happy meeting."

IV

The prestige of Lady Hamilton was high in Naples, where she was the confidante and bosom friend of the Queen. She had now, for fifteen years, reigned as hostess at the Palazzo Sessa, where three large likenesses of her, by Romney, adorned the dining-room. Her doting husband had bought pictures of her as a model, in her teens (in a pink silk gown and a big black hat), as a Bacchante (with auburn tresses flying), and as St. Cecilia (looking heavenwards). There was no question that since her marriage she had been a perfectly faithful wife, though moving in a depraved society. Nelson's fortieth birthday took place on September 29th. Eighteen hundred guests were invited to a ball and supper at the British Embassy, and the rejoicings were marred by an ugly outburst from the Admiral's stepson. Captain Josiah Nisbet, pointing at Lady Hamilton and Nelson, shouted, " That woman is ruining that man! " He was quickly removed by the burly Troubridge and other blue-coats, and he was demonstrably drunk, but the fact remained that he was expressing a belief which was to grow amongst those to whom Nelson's reputation was dearest. Exactly a week had passed since his arrival in Naples, and already concerned friends were noticing that he was displaying every sign of a lad in his first affair. He blushed when his hostess literally, and very loudly, sang his praises (in an extra verse appended to the National Anthem). He embarrassed casual audiences by remarking upon her singular abilities and accomplishments, only surpassed by her boundless kindness of heart. When Lord St. Vincent was informed that Lady Hamilton was an Angel, he received the information with his usual calm, but a further confidence, dated October 5th, alarmed him:

> " I am writing opposite Lady Hamilton, therefore you will not be surprised at the glorious jumble of this letter. Were your Lordship in my place, I much doubt if you could write so well; our hearts and hands must be all in a flutter. Naples is a dangerous place, and we must keep clear of it."

Duty called, and he did keep clear of Naples, but not for long, for duty unquestionably called him back, and it happened that his sudden appearances and disappearances took place against backgrounds that were highly romantic. He dashed off to superintend the blockade of Malta, took the little island of Goza, and returned to tell Ferdinand of Naples that he was now the sovereign of sixteen thousand new subjects. His Majesty of the Two Sicilies, much prodded by his wife and Lady Hamilton, had now made a treaty of alliance with Austria and declared war on France. Nelson met the Austrian General Mack, first at the amazing country palace of Caserta (where the Hamiltons translated between a General who understood no Italian and an Admiral who spoke English only), and next, under starry skies in the tented field, whence Ferdinand at length departed, to enter Rome in triumph. But when Nelson anchored in Naples Bay on December 5th after a very rough passage, to report the unconditional surrender of Leghorn, he found that Ferdinand's officers, as he had suspected, " did not like fighting." An army of from forty to fifty thousand men had bolted " like rabbits," said the despairing Queen, almost without firing a shot at twelve thousand French advancing towards Naples. In their defence, it must be admitted that one of the first to slip back to Naples in civilian disguise had been His Majesty. A mob which seemed to the Queen to resemble that which had dragged the royal family of France back to Paris, yelled outside her palace until reassured by bowings and smilings from a balcony. At the Palazzo Sessa, Sir William Hamilton was packing his antiquities, and his wife was sitting up nightly to receive a mysterious and unending stream of casks, crates and packages, delivered by British seamen and marines, and labelled " Stores for Nelson." These contained personal property of their Majesties, reckoned by the Admiral to be worth £2,500,000.

Less than a fortnight after his return from Leghorn he had written to the British Minister at Constantinople, " I do not know whether the whole Royal Family, with 3,000 Neapolitan émigrés, will not be under the protection of the King's flag this night." The embarkation began on the night of December 21st. Amongst reasons for postponement had been the problem of how to get the party unobserved from the palace to the landing-stage on a minor quay. This was solved by the recollection that amongst the amenities of the Palazzo Reale was a secret passage. Nelson dined at the British Embassy, and drove on to attend a reception offered by the Turkish Ambassador, who had come to invest him personally with the gifts sent from the Porte by the Grand Signior—a sable pelisse, and a diamond ornament called a " Chelengk," taken from one of the Imperial turbans. The Hamiltons and Nelson withdrew early from Kelim Effendi's entertainment, on foot, and hurried to their appointed posts. Lady Hamilton's task was to support the Queen, who was in a hysterical condition, and escort her and her family down the long subterranean tunnel leading to the landing-stage. Nelson, having come himself with the barges and cutters which were to carry them out to his Fleet, sped up the passage to meet them, " my mind never better and my heart in the right trim." The extremely foul weather which had added to the horrors of the day had abated, but the appearance of Naples Bay was enough to shock passengers much less pusillanimous than the Neapolitan royal family.

The first batch of seasick refugees came on board the *Vanguard* between 9.30 and 10 p.m. The Admiral's quarters had been prepared for the ladies and children; gentlemen were directed to the wardroom. Soon, the flagship, rolling at single anchor, became a scene of confusion and overcrowding, and dawn brought a storm so violent that no communication could take place between ships. On December 23rd the *Vanguard* weighed and made sail at 7 p.m. in company with one British 74 and three transports, a single Neapolitan corvette and about a score of merchant vessels. "Next day," Nelson recorded, "it blew harder than I have ever experienced since I have been at sea." Tom Allen, in his element, had told the shattered ladies of title occupying his master's premises that they would be all right, "while the sticks stand." When they heard seamen with axes pattering to cut away the wreck of the ship's top-sails, they concluded that they had escaped being torn in pieces by a revolutionary mob, only to be drowned. The King's confessor, flung from his crib, sustained a fractured forearm. The Duchess of Castelcicala cut her head on Admiral Nelson's sideboard. On Christmas Day, Prince Alberto, aged six, died of convulsions in the arms of Lady Hamilton. Her behaviour from the moment she had come on board a British man-of-war had been such as to increase every man's admiration.

She had set an example of the highest courage and unselfishness—given up her bedding and linen to her fellow sufferers and devoted herself to unceasing attendance upon them. Nelson believed that " Good Sir William also made every sacrifice," but according to one of his officers, her ladyship, at the height of the gale, had discovered her elderly husband sitting apart in his cabin with a loaded pistol in each hand. " He was resolved not to die with the ' guggle-guggle-guggle ' of the salt water in his throat; and therefore he was prepared, as soon as he felt the ship sinking, to shoot himself! "

The *Vanguard* anchored safely within Palermo mole early on the morning of December 27th, and the arrival of Ferdinand in his second capital was greeted with apparent rejoicing.

* 5 *

"Rinaldo in the Arms of Armida"

PALERMO IN the early weeks of 1799 struck the refugees from Naples very unfavourably. The gratitude of the King and Queen had caused them to present to Nelson and the Hamiltons a palace designed for summer holiday weather. The Villa Bastioni did not possess a single fireplace. Sir William, too old to be moved in such weather from a home where he had lived in comfort for thirty-five years (and deeply mourning his collection of antiques), took to his bed. Lady Hamilton, now that the heroic hour had passed, naturally wept for the loss of her town house, the " Villa Emma," six or seven equipages and most of her wardrobe. Nelson was kept warm by a letter from Commodore Sir Sidney Smith, who wrote to say that he had been appointed to a combined naval and diplomatic post in the Levant, was going to conduct operations in Egypt and had been allowed by their Lordships to choose Captain Miller as his second-in-command. Nelson's furious comment to St. Vincent bore fruit, but not immediately, and although Sir Sidney was eventually obliged to relinquish his broad pendant, and the First Lord admitted " very great misunderstanding," a vain and disappointed man remained a thorn in Nelson's flesh while he continued in the Mediterranean.

Until April, all the news coming into Palermo was unmitigatedly bad, for the French, welcomed by many collaborators in high places, had taken possession of Naples and established a republic named "the Parthenopæan," with triumphant ease. The only hope of the exiles was a counter-revolution, and meanwhile their situation at Palermo was not happy. Loyal Sicilians were disgusted by the King's preference for the counsellors who had come with him from Naples, and by the fact that he seemed to have no plans for the future except the establishment of several new hunting lodges. Nelson described himself, in letters home, as " not to be envied," and said that he hoped soon to be released from his attendance on so wretched a court. In early February he read out he had been promoted from Rear-Admiral of the Blue to Rear-Admiral of the White, but his domestic news was wholly dispiriting. His wife was no longer living in the house he had bought for her. It was damp. She had moved to Bath while it was renovated. Uncle William Suckling of Kentish Town had died, leaving Sir Horatio Nelson an executor, with a legacy of £100. It was Nelson's sad duty to report to his lady that her son was not developing favourably. " I am sorry to say, with real grief, that he has nothing good about him. He must—sooner or later—be broke, and I am sure neither you nor I can help it." A suggestion that

Lady Nelson should come out " to join the Standard at Naples," forwarded by Davison, who seemed to have been hearing gossip, was not encouraged. " I could, if you had come, *only* have struck my flag and carried you back again . . . It is probable that I shall yet be home in the summer."

But as the weather improved, the political outlook also became brighter. A combined Turkish and Russian squadron captured Corfu. In his native Calabria, leading an army composed mostly of peasants and brigands, Cardinal Fabrizio Ruffo was causing considerable anxiety to the occupying French, who were finding their new conquest much more difficult to hold down than they had been led to expect. Troubridge, who had been blockading the coast, was ordered to get in touch with the royalists in Naples. He re-took the lovely pumice islands in the immediate neighbourhood—Procida, Ischia . . . (" Your Lordship never beheld such loyalty "), and wrote urgently asking that their Majesties would send Neapolitan troops and an honest judge. Loyalists were delivering to his squadron all of their compatriots whom they deemed deserved death for collaboration. Their Majesties, who had bickered throughout the winter, seemed agreed that they must not venture back to Naples till it was " entirely cleansed," and that they must be protected by Nelson. The judge sent by them was summed up by Troubridge as the poorest creature he ever saw, " frightened out of his senses." The General refused to land his troops. Troubridge realised that the odium for anything that aroused criticism would be thrown upon Nelson's squadron. " I desired the General and all his cowardly gang to get out of a British man-of-war. We want people to fight; he does not come under that description. I told him plainly that his King will never do well until he has hanged half his officers."

The case of Commodore Caracciolo was typical. He was one of those who had followed Ferdinand to Palermo; but in February he had returned to the mainland, on the plea that he must protect his estates. Ferdinand's farewell to him had struck a warning note—" Beware of meddling with French politics . . . I know I shall recover my kingdom of Naples." By mid-May the only French troops left in Naples were those garrisoning the castle of St. Elmo; but Caracciolo had not made the speedy return to Palermo which he had promised. The deserted authorities of the Parthenopæan Republic had begged him to take charge of a flotilla of gunboats which had been formed to check the activity of the British men-of-war at Procida. On one occasion, coming into action against the Sicilian frigate *Minerva*, he had fired upon her. She had once been his own flagship. The Queen of Naples wrote imperiously to Cardinal Ruffo:

" I say it with sorrow, but those who have served the King, as, for instance Caracciolo . . . and have been found fighting against him, with arms in their hands, are deserving of the death penalty."

Nelson arrived in Naples Bay in a fine new second-rate, H.M.S. *Foudroyant*, on the afternoon of June 24th, to find flags of truce flying from the sea-forts of Uovo and Nuovo (held by the Neapolitan Jacobins), from St. Elmo, and on H.M.S. *Seahorse* (Captain Foote). Lord Keith, who had now succeeded Lord St. Vincent as Chief in the Mediterranean, believed the Combined Fleets of France and Spain to be bound either for Naples or Sicily. On his passage, Nelson had learned that Ruffo, sickened by the murderous excesses of his own troops, and panic-stricken by the news of the Combined Fleets being at sea, had concluded a three-weeks' Armistice with the rebels. Captain Foote, in charge of the British flotilla, explained when he came on board the Admiral to report, that the document to which he had unwillingly put his name, yesterday, following the example of the Cardinal and the Russian naval commander, was, so far as Ferdinand's disloyal subjects were concerned, no Armistice. It was a definite capitulation. He admitted unhappily that he had thought its terms very favourable, for they were to be allowed to march out with the honours of war, and with all their property. Nelson told him that he had blundered ("been imposed upon by that worthless fellow Cardinal Ruffo, who was endeavouring to form a party hostile to the interests of his Sovereign "), annulled what he believed to be an Armistice by a signal, and anchored his fleet in a close line of battle before the city. He demanded unconditional surrender from the French, and told the Neapolitan

Jacobins that he would not allow them to leave
Nuovo and Uovo.

Next day he had a furious interview with the
" swelled-up priest " whom he mistrusted, at which,
when Sir William Hamilton retired worn out from
the duties of interpreter, his wife took his place.
Convinced after a weary tussle that " an Admiral is
no match in talking with a Cardinal," Nelson sent
his guest off with a document in which he declared
that the Treaty which he found had been entered
into ought not to be executed without the consent
of His Sicilian Majesty, Earl St. Vincent and Lord
Keith. Next morning Sir William sent Ruffo a line
saying that Nelson would wait for instructions from
Palermo; but the Jacobins in the sea-forts, justly
nervous of falling into the hands of Ruffo's irregulars,
or the curious and powerful band of Neapolitan
beggars, the " lazzaroni " always faithful to Ferdinand, surrendered before the day was out.

By June 28th the desired instructions from Palermo
arrived—" no conditions except unconditional surrender "—and Nelson sent Foote to explain to Acton
that it was " a toss-up " whether or not he arrested
Ruffo, and that he must beg that the King and *Queen*
(thrice underlined) hastened to the scene. While he
was trying to " keep things tolerable " until their
arrival, Commodore Caracciolo was brought on
board the *Foudroyant* in handcuffs by triumphant
Calabrian soldiers. He had fled from one of the sea-
forts, and taken refuge in disguise upon the estate of

a relative. A warning that he had been betrayed had caused him to leave a villa for a hut, and finally the depths of a well. Determined to choose a glaring case for an example of the " quick punishments and speedy rewards " which he had always urged upon their Majesties as the only basis of good government, Nelson ordered the senior Neapolitan officer present to assemble a court martial. Caracciolo was found guilty and condemned to death. The proceedings were conducted in Italian and Nelson was not present; but upon hearing the verdict he ordered that it should be carried out on the same evening, and that after the Commodore had been hanged at the foreyard arm of *La Minerva*, which he had once commanded, his body should be cut down and cast into the sea.

Jacobins, and their friends, throughout Europe, succeeded in raising a violent clamour, and persuading many that an English Admiral had been guilty of breach of faith and murder. He was accused of having treacherously obtained possession of the garrisons of the forts by means of a capitulation, and in violation of its terms having slaughtered Caracciolo and many others. The executions which dragged on for months after the arrival of the King and Queen were barbarous and horrible (they had been very badly frightened), but not until the following May did Nelson hear any criticism of his actions. On the contrary, he received meanwhile congratulations on his success from the First Lord, and from Ferdinand the title of Duke of Brontë in Sicily and Knight Grand

Cross of the Order of St. Ferdinand and Merit. But until Commander Jefferson Miles took up the pen in his defence, in 1843, the often repeated inaccuracies of Captain Foote, Miss Helen Maria Williams, and even Robert Southey, Poet Laureate, had convinced many saddened readers that Nelson under the spell of Lady Hamilton, " a wicked siren," confidante of a bloodthirsty and immoral queen, had acted towards a blameless Neapolitan sea-officer with ill-faith, precipitance and cruelty.

II

On the afternoon of Sunday, November 9th, 1800, the worst thunderstorm known for nearly a hundred years broke over London. Outside Nerot's Hotel, in St. James's Street, a reporter was waiting, and in the hall the Reverend Edmund and Lady Nelson. The Admiral had landed at Yarmouth after a very rough passage in the mail-packet from Cuxhaven, on Thursday. The failure of the Government to send a frigate to fetch home the Victor of the Nile had been resented in his native Norfolk. Volunteers had dragged his carriage up to The Wrestler's Arms, and a band had struck up a national air as he appeared on the balcony of the well-known inn. By his side had stood Lady Hamilton, in a muslin gown embroidered with the words " Nelson " and " Brontë."

His behaviour since the summer of 1799 had not earned the approbation of Lord Keith, or the Admiralty.

His refusal to send a single ship to protect Minorca
had been justified in fact. ("It is better to save the
Kingdom of Naples and risk Minorca, than to risk the
Kingdom of Naples and save Minorca.") On receiving
a second order he had detached a strong squadron,
and Minorca had not been threatened. But with his
temporary appointment to the command left vacant
by Keith's withdrawal to the Atlantic and Baltic, he
had received a stinging rebuke from Whitehall, "a
severe set-down." It was true that in attaching himself
so indefatigably to the Royal Neapolitan interest he
was acting under previous instructions; but except for
a fortnight in October, when he visited Port Mahon,
he was continually at Palermo, and when Keith, on
his return, offered him Syracuse, Augusta or Messina
as a more convenient rendezvous from which to conduct the blockade of Malta, his response was a request
for a fortnight's sick-leave "to go to my friends at
Palermo." He had found a large villa—the Palazzo
Palagonia, which he shared with the Hamiltons.
Captain Ball found that Lady Hamilton "fascinated all
the Navy" as much, in this luxurious setting, as she
had done at the Palazzo Sessa, but Troubridge was
maddened by tales that supper parties at which Nelson
was joint-host were enlivened by high play at Faro.

Palermo had now become very gay. There was a
much-publicised fête in September offered by the
Queen in honour of her British friends, at which
the Admiral, accompanied by "Lady Hamilton,
Britannia's pride," was observed to walk about wearing

a wreath of laurel. This was followed, a month later, by a Chinese fête which " really outdid the Arabian Nights " and was said to have cost £6,000. Lady Elgin, wife of the British Ambassador *en route* for the Porte, thought that Nelson looked very ill—" quite dying, and yet as if he had no other thought than her . . . He is now completely managed by Lady Hamilton."

From a house in South Audley Street, on a dark November day, old Admiral Goodall wrote with his usual bluntness, " They say here you are Rinaldo in the arms of Armida, and that it requires the firmness of an Ubaldo and his brother knight to draw you from the Enchantress." Nelson knew now that the last of the ships-of-the-line which had escaped him at the Nile had been captured by his squadron. He wrote sadly:

" My task is done, my health is lost, and the orders of the great Earl of St. Vincent are completely fulfilled. I hope the *Foudroyant* will be able to come here, to carry us first to Malta, and from thence, taking the Queen of Naples to Leghorn, proceed with us, at least to Gibraltar, if not to England."

He sailed for Malta in April, taking the Hamiltons with him, but according to the British Consul at Leghorn, Keith had added to his refusal of anything more than a frigate or a troopship for their passage home, the remark that " Lady Hamilton had had command of the Fleet long enough." The First Lord expressed his regret that the state of Lord Nelson's

Plate 3 Lord Nelson. Pastel by J. H. Schmidt

Plate 4 Lady Hamilton. Pastel by J. H. Schmidt

health had obliged him to quit his station off Malta. Should the enemy come suddenly into the Mediterranean, Lord Spencer would be concerned to hear that Admiral Nelson had learned of this, either on shore, or in a transport at Palermo. Without wishing to recall him he believed that he would be best advised to come home at once rather than remain " inactive at a foreign Court."

The party decided to travel home overland, through Italy, Austria and Germany, and enjoyed a triumphal progress, occupying a little more than four months. In Vienna, Lady Minto presented Lady Hamilton at the Imperial Court, and was vexed that Nelson appeared " a gig from ribands, orders and stars," but had to admit that " his honest simple manners " were completely unchanged. In Dresden, the British Minister called in to help him to entertain " Antony and Moll Cleopatra," a young Irish widow, with the incredibly romantic name of Mrs. Melesina St. George. The criticisms of this lady, herself an authoress, musician and beauty, were destined to be repeated in every Nelson biography. She found Sir William's affectation of youthful agility pitiful, Lord Nelson " a willing captive " and Lady Hamilton " more stamped with the manners of her first situation than one would suppose." To her host she confided alarm at the quantity of champagne enjoyed by the astonishing trio. The journalist who watched them arrive at Nerot's Hotel had a more indulgent pen. He noted that the Admiral, though thin, looked extremely well in full uniform, wearing two medals and two stars. Lady Hamilton attended by a black *femme de chambre*, " Fatima," " looked charmingly, and is a very fine woman." Sir William, like his fellow K.B., appeared at the end of so long a journey " thin in person."

On that dark and uneasy November evening in a London hotel, while distant thunder groaned and winds sighed, Lady Nelson began to appreciate something of which she had been amply warned, " the wonderful change, past belief." The millionaire William Beckford had offered the Hamiltons his house in Grosvenor Square, and Davison, in preparation for Nelson's return, had taken, for the Admiral and family, a large house in Dover Street. But although they were no longer under the same roof, the inseparable friends met daily. There was a scene after Nelson's own heart when he arrived at the Lord Mayor's Banquet, dragged by the cheering populace from Ludgate Hill to the Guildhall doors. " The illustrious Tar, landing from his carriage," shook hands warmly with several " old Agamemnons," and afterwards conducted to his station, under a triumphal arch, " hoisted the sword of the value of two hundred guineas " voted to him by the City, and repeated his promise that he hoped soon to use it. At St. James's Palace his reception was not so encouraging, and he arrived to a Service dinner-party at Admiralty House, to which the Hamiltons were not invited, looking like thunder. Lady Spencer, who had been surprised on the last occasion that she entertained the Nelsons by a request that a husband might sit next a wife of whom he saw too little, announced after this evening, " Such a contrast I never beheld! " During dessert, Lady Nelson " perhaps inadvisedly, but with good intention," prepared for a one-armed man a wine-glass filled with peeled walnuts. He pushed it aside so impatiently that it hit a plate and was shattered. . . . Lady Nelson had burst into tears at the First Lord's table. . . . She had fainted in a box at Drury Lane. The Admiral had gone to spend Christmas at Beckford's country house without her, but with, of course, the Hamiltons. . . . London seethed with gossip, which was reflected in some remarkably ugly cartoons, displayed in St. James's Street. A young solicitor, Mr. William Haslewood, always claimed to have been present at a fatal breakfast in Dover Street from which Lady Nelson arose, and with the words " I am sick of hearing of dear Lady Hamilton," swept out of the room, and her husband's life. " She never made any apology for her abrupt and ungentle conduct above related, or any overtures towards a reconciliation." That the unhappy couple, who parted on January 13th, 1801, never met again is a fact, but it is equally certain that neither as yet guessed that they had said their last farewell. Nelson sent a line reporting his arrival at Southampton the same night, and Lady Nelson continued to address him for a year, suggesting a fresh start.

But a fact of which she was unaware had loaded the dice against her. On February 1st, in Torbay,

Nelson got some news from London for which he had been waiting in frantic impatience and anxiety. A cryptic note told him that Lady Hamilton was well. He was the father of a daughter. Cynics had drawn their own conclusions as to the passion which he had displayed so ingenuously, almost from the hour of his arrival at Naples from the Nile. But they much under-estimated the duration of his struggle between love and duty. This had continued from September, 1798, until February, 1800. ("Ah! my dear friend, I did well remember the 12th February, and also the two months afterwards. I never shall forget them and never be sorry for the consequences.") As soon as possible he took post-chaise for London and three days' leave, "almost beside himself with expectation." He saw Lady Hamilton, and Davison. He also visited a Mrs. Gibson, of 9 Little Titchfield Street, Marylebone, a respectable widow in poor circumstances, who had asked no awkward questions when "Hond: Lady Hamilton" unattended, in a hackney coach, had arrived to deliver to her care an infant not more than eight days old, "Horatia Thompson," the orphan of one of Lord Nelson's young sea-officers, and his lordship's god-child.

Some of those who loved Nelson best protested to the last that the devotion for another man's wife, which he exhibited so openly, was innocent, that "the attraction between her and our hero was something of a kindred enthusiasm in the cause of their Country." The question remained unsolved until 1893, when

Mr. Alfred Morrison, connoisseur and antiquarian, bought at Sotheby's a collection of hundreds of letters in the handwriting of Nelson, some of which, as they had been entrusted to private messengers, were entirely unguarded. One, dated Torbay, March 1st, opened, " Now, my own dear wife, for such you are in my eyes, and in the face of heaven, I can give full scope to my feelings . . . I love, I never did love any-one else. I never had a dear pledge of love till you gave me one, and you, thank my God, never gave one to anybody else."

His " non-pareil " had told him as much as she dared of her story. He knew that Sir William's nephew, Greville, " that other chap," had used her ill enough. It does not appear that he ever knew that a younger Emma, the fruit of a very early indiscretion, was already nineteen when Horatia was born.

Nelson's love-letters of early 1801, sometimes Shakespearian in cadence, reminiscent of the ravings of Othello or Leontes, are terrible reading. He was racked with remorse and with groundless jealousy, notably of the libertine Prince of Wales, who had chosen this inauspicious date to mention " how Lady Hamilton had struck his fancy." In his wildest moments, " poor Jack, shut up in wood," even proposed that, taking with them " our dear little child," Lady Hamilton and he should fly to eternal exile on his estate of Brontë.

* 6 *

Copenhagen

NELSON'S PROMOTION to Vice-Admiral of the Blue had been gazetted on New Year's Day, but St. Vincent had sent to the Admiralty a very unpromising description of his present state of mind. It was as second-in-command to Sir Hyde Parker, an undistinguished officer, that he sailed from Yarmouth on March 12th, 1801, to engage in service against the Northern Confederation, the armed neutrality of the Baltic. Sir Hyde, " a little nervous about dark nights and fields of ice," had struck his pen through every recommendation made by the Victor of the Nile and shown him no confidence. All Nelson knew when he put to sea was that all the newspapers and Yarmouth fisherwomen said that the Fleet, amounting to fifty-three sail, was going to wait outside Cronenburg while the British Minister in Copenhagen negotiated. (" I disapprove most exceedingly . . . Weak in the extreme . . . A fleet of British men-of-war are the best negotiators in Europe . . .")

Fog as thick as mud had been all that was visible as his squadron struggled up from Spithead, and as the Fleet battled its way northwards, ice shone upon the rigging and sleet storms gave place to snowstorms. On March 15th, Lord Nelson in the *St. George* and Captain Fremantle in the *Ganges* sadly and grimly laid aside unfinished letters. The draught in the Admiral's Great Cabin was enough to turn a mill, and in the *Ganges* the hacking coughs of the ship's company formed a perpetual distraction. Early on the 18th, a low, grey, sandy peninsula became visible, through flying snowflakes; the Fleet collected, and presently turned southwards down the Kattegat. A second duty-call upon Sir Hyde " ground out something," but not until the 23rd, when they had lain at anchor for three days eighteen miles out from the defences of Cronenburg and Elsinore, with the wind fair for Copenhagen, did the Chief call a council. At this " all the heads were very gloomy." The diplomatic mission had been a failure. When Nelson arrived it had been decided that to stay where they were until the Danes, Russians and Swedes came forth to offer battle, was the only prudent course. The Danes were far too much frightened of Russia to consent to the suggestion that they should withdraw from the Confederation. They were actively hostile. Sir Hyde's " thunderbolt " second-in-command began by questioning the nego-tiators as to the strength and position of the enemy. If it was correct that the Danes had placed their strongest ships at the head of their line, there were possibilities in a surprise attack from the rear. This would mean an entry into the Baltic by the Great Belt, which must entail loss of time. His own plan of

campaign would have been to send a squadron
through the Belt and up the Baltic to deal first with
the Russians at Revel, while the remainder of the
Fleet reduced, or at least held in check, the Danes at
Copenhagen. Paul of Russia he regarded as the trunk
of the League, the Swedes and Danes as mere branches.
If the trunk fell, so did the branches; but branches
might be lopped off, leaving a trunk still standing.
Sir Hyde, however, was loath to leave a strong enemy
in his rear, and it said much for Nelson's eloquence
that by the time the council broke up, even an approach
by the Great Belt had been decided upon.

On his return to his own ship he wrote to the Commander-in-Chief, reviewing the alternative plans of
attack, and strongly representing that the boldest
measures were the safest. His proposal was that he
should be sent with a squadron of ten smaller ships-
of-the-line, frigates and other vessels of light draught,
to pass between the Middle Ground, the shoal opposite the capital, and the Saltholm flats. He would
then assail the southern end of the Danish line—the
hulks, gun and bomb vessels covering the city front,
while the remainder of the British Fleet engaged the
powerful Trekroner (Three Crowns) battery at the
northern end.

But caution was amongst Sir Hyde's strong points.
On the 26th he still thought it necessary that he
should send a message to Governor Stricker of Elsinore,
inquiring his intentions if a British Fleet were to pass
the Sound. A couple of young Danish officers came

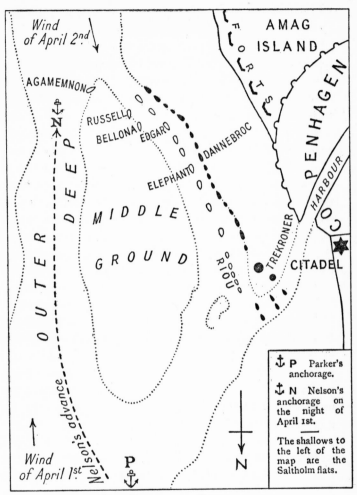

THE BATTLE OF COPENHAGEN

on board the Chief's flagship, and one of them called out, " Admiral, if your guns are no better than your pens, you may as well return to England! " But on hearing the name of the second-in-command he was much struck. " What, is he here? I would give a hundred guineas to see him! Then I suppose it is no joke, if he is come? "

The fort at Cronenburg could not permit him to pass, so Sir Hyde interpreted this to his satisfaction as a declaration of war, and the wind coming fair, the stately British flotilla achieved the passage through the narrows with perfect ease. The Swedes did not open fire from Helsingborg, so they kept close to the Swedish coast while Cronenburg blazed away ineffectively. Nelson, meanwhile, had changed from the *St. George*, a three-decker, into a 74, H.M.S. *Elephant*, commanded by Foley (who had led inside the French line in Aboukir Bay), and on the afternoon of the day in which he came in sight of Copenhagen he embarked with a party of senior officers in a lugger to reconnoitre the harbour and channels. Under his personal supervision, amongst floating ice-blocks during the hours of darkness, British masters and pilots began to place the buoys necessary to guide his squadron. His opinion of the sullen and solid line of enemy defence was, " It looks formidable to those who are children at War, but to my judgment, with ten sail-of-the-line, I think I can annihilate them; at all events I hope to be allowed to try." Next afternoon he had to fight for the desired permission, for Sir Hyde was, very reasonably, alarmed at the prospect; but once his decision was taken he acted handsomely. He offered two more of-the-line than Nelson had asked for, and thenceforward left all matters to his direction.

On the morning of April 1st, Nelson made a final examination in the *Amazon* frigate (Captain Riou), and when he gave the signal to weigh (which was received with three cheers in every ship) the frigate led his division down the Outer Channel to moor at the southern end of the Middle Ground. As the *Elephant* dropped her anchor, he called out loudly, " I will fight them the moment I have a fair wind." Late that evening he sat down to dine with comrades in arms whose names would hereafter be remembered together with his own. The signal to prepare for battle had been given. He was noted to be in the highest spirits as he drank to a leading wind and to the success of the following day.

He had his cot placed that night in a position on the deck from which he could dictate to a posse of secretaries, and during the small hours, when reports of the wind coming fair were brought in to him, he urged them to hurry their pens. He was dressed before six, but after his Captains had received their instructions, and the pilots came on board, an unforeseen difficulty arose. " At 8 a.m. o'clock on the morning of April 2nd, . . . I experienced the misery of having the honour of our Country intrusted to pilots who had no other thought than to keep the ships clear of danger, and their own silly heads clear of shot." At last the Master of the *Bellona*, a veteran of the Nile, volunteered; the signal to weigh in succession was thrown out at 9.30, and " the *Edgar* proceeded in a noble manner for the channel." " Not a word was spoken through the ship save by the pilot and the helmsman, and their commands, being chanted very much in the same manner as the responses in a cathedral service, added to the solemnity."

II

The Battle of Copenhagen opened with a series of mishaps. The *Agamemnon*, followed by the *Edgar*, could not weather the shoals at the head of the channel, and never came into action. The *Polyphemus*, taking up her station promptly, was very roughly handled. The *Isis*, *Glatton* and *Ardent* were successful in occupying the berths assigned to them, but the *Bellona* grounded, and the *Russell*, losing sight of her leader in the smoke of battle, shared her fate. From the outset Nelson's division was reduced from twelve to nine of-the-line, and the gunnery of the Danes was superior to his expectations. His concern was extreme as the *Agamemnon* signalled inability to proceed, and two further 74s failed to obey his orders to engage more closely. But he kept the signal to advance flying. He starboarded the *Elephant's* helm, passed to larboard between the grounded ships and the enemy line, and made for the position left vacant by the *Bellona*. As the *Ganges* passed, he hailed Fremantle to place her as close as possible ahead of his flagship. The only men in the *Ganges* to be hit before she anchored, happened to be the master and pilot. Fremantle himself carried his ship in. The *Monarch* dropped into the berth originally intended for Nelson's flagship, and by seventeen minutes past eleven the action had become general, each ship as she arrived opposite to her number in the Danish line, anchoring by the stern and presenting her broadside. Graves in the *Defiance* was the last to take up his position, ahead of the *Monarch*, who had lost her Captain. Owing to the accidents to three of his 74s, the Trekroner was going unmarked. Nelson sent in Riou with his squadron of small craft to attack it. There was no sign of Sir Hyde, who should have been appearing to make a menacing appearance from the north. He was still four miles distant, beating up against Nelson's fair wind.

About one o'clock the Commander-in-Chief, who could see little of what was happening, but realised that Nelson was in trouble, wished to discontinue the action. His Flag-Captain obtained permission to go on board the *Elephant* to investigate, but before he reached her Sir Hyde had acted. Nelson, at 1.30, was walking the starboard side of his quarter-deck. The *Elephant* was engaging the Danish flagship *Dannebrog* and two floating batteries. As a shot passed through the mainmast of the *Elephant*, causing a shower of splinters, Nelson remarked to Lieutenant-

Colonel the Hon. William Stewart, who was waiting to land his troops, that this was " warm work." When Sir Hyde's signal was reported to him, he continued his walk. The Signal Lieutenant, meeting him at the next turn, asked whether he should repeat the signal to the squadron. Nelson told him to acknowledge it, but keep " Number 16 " (for close action) still flying. Stewart noticed that the Admiral was now moving and speaking with increased speed and working the stump of his right arm. " Do you know what's shown on board of the Commander-in-Chief ? Number 39." The Colonel had to admit ignorance. " Why, to leave off action . . . Leave off action! Now damn me if I do." He gave a shrug, and turning to Foley, said, " You know, Foley, I have only one eye. I have a right to be blind sometimes." He raised his spy-glass to his right eye, and announced. " I really do not see the signal."

III

About 2 p.m. when Fremantle came on board the Admiral, the Danish ships astern of the flagship had been silenced, and gunboats and batteries were floating helplessly from the enemy line. The Great Cabin of the *Elephant* was filled with strange uniforms to whom Lord Nelson was expressing his detestation of Russia. He thrust into Fremantle's hand a note on which he asked his opinion.

" To the Brothers of Englishmen, the Danes.

Lord Nelson has direction to spare Denmark, when no longer resisting, but if the firing is continued on the part of Denmark, Lord Nelson will be obliged to set on fire all the Floating-batteries he has taken, without having the power of saving the brave Danes who have defended them."

Fremantle and Foley pointed out that the Admiral had several ships aground, and that those engaged were mostly so crippled that it would be wise to remove them from a very difficult channel while the wind was favourable. Captain Frederick Thesiger (late of the Russian service) was sent off in a flag of truce, to find the Crown Prince (regent for an imbecile sire), who was " animating his countrymen in a spirited manner." During his absence the leading men-of-war of Sir Hyde's division began to appear, and the remainder of the Danish ships ahead of the *Elephant* surrendered. The *Dannebrog*, in which there had been great carnage, had broken from her moorings and was drifting in flames before the wind, spreading terror and confusion along the Danish line. Only four ships in Copenhagen harbour, the Trekroner, and a battery on Amag island were still firing, and half of their shot was unavoidably reaching such of their own hulks as had already struck. As Adjutant-General Lindholm passed the Trekroner, on his way to ask Admiral Nelson, on behalf of the Prince, " the particular object of sending his flag of truce," he ordered the battery to cease fire, whereupon the *Elephant* made the same signal to her division.

The Battle of Copenhagen closed about 4 p.m. Nelson ordered his gig, and prepared to follow Lindholm to conference in the *London*. As he embarked Stewart heard him say, " Well, I have fought contrary to orders and perhaps I shall be hanged." Physical exhaustion may have been taking its toll as he was pulled four miles in sunset light through a scene of desolation towards his Commander-in-Chief. He seemed to his companions to be in low spirits. Graves, unable to make out his response to Parker's signal of recall, had therefore repeated it, and the gallant Riou, hauling off his light craft with the words, " What will Nelson think of us? " had been cut in two by a shot from the Trekroner. Thompson of the *Bellona* had lost a leg. Both the *Elephant* and *Defiance* had run aground when attempting to obey the signal to weigh in succession.

But Nelson was, in fact, deep sunk in thought how best to secure by negotiation what he had won to-day by force. A twenty-four-hours' truce was agreed upon that night, and it was suggested that Sir Hyde's second-in-command should go on shore to converse with His Royal Highness. Nelson returned to the *St. George* to sleep, but before he slept he wrote to Lady Hamilton to tell her that, " of eighteen sail, large and small some are taken, some sunk, some burnt, in the good old way." He enclosed a verse, entitled *Lord Nelson to his Guardian Angel*, endorsed " St. George,

April 2nd, 1801, at 9 o'clock at night very tired after a hard fought battle."

IV

He had said of himself, " A negotiator is certainly out of my line," but the fourteen weeks' Armistice carried through cheering crowds by Commissioners from the Amalienborg Palace towards the British Commander-in-Chief's flagship on April 9th was the result of some hard tussling on his part. " All here hang on my shoulders." He had been obliged to state that he was ready to renew hostilities at any moment. When he had stumped for the last time out of a Scandinavian royal residence which, he had muttered, " would burn very well," he was " tired to death." The Danish Prince's advisers were also heaving sighs of relief. They had just heard that Paul of Russia had been murdered on the morning of March 25th. Nelson's comment on this was that he did not believe he would have to fire another shot in the Baltic, and he was right, but ten days later a message from Sir Hyde, that a look-out frigate had seen the Swedish Fleet at sea, sent him off at 6 p.m. on a sharp night, prepared to cover a distance of some fifty leagues in an open boat, to join the British Fleet at anchor. Fortunately it had not sailed, and when the Captain of the *Elephant* recognised a voice he knew well inquiring " in true Norfolk drawl," whether he could be so good as to be plagued by Admiral Nelson again, his response was warm. Sir Hyde's Fleet proceeded in a leisurely manner towards Carlskrona to find eight Swedish sail-of-the-line and two frigates " very snug," shut up in their fine harbour from which Nelson was sure that they would not venture out again this summer.

By May 5th he awaited only the arrival of a despatch vessel with his orders to come home. When it appeared, to their dismay, Sir Hyde, who had been well pleased with his situation, found himself recalled. Nelson, who was already in spirit in England, was appointed to succeed him. He sent Lady Hamilton a line urging her to cheer up, " I am on my way to Russia," and sailed for Revel. To his disappointment, he found that the twelve sail-of-the-line which had been ice-bound there, had got out a week before and gone up to Cronstadt. French-speaking Russian officers came on board his flagship and he saw that affairs had now entered the realms of diplomacy. Count Pahlen, on behalf of Alexander I, announced his Imperial master's dismay that the whole fleet of a nation expressing friendly intentions should have come into the Gulf of Finland. The signal to weigh was immediately thrown out by the *St. George*, and Nelson took his Fleet down to Rostock. There he lay, for a month, refusing all invitations to land, disgusted that Sir Hyde had prevented him from vanquishing the Russians, and depressed by " the influenza " and the improbability of his seeing any service in these waters. He had written to the influential Davison to tell him to do all that he could to get him relieved of a most unwelcome command, and also to deliver an ultimatum to Lady Nelson. The sum of £1,200 which she would receive annually was a separation allowance, " For sooner than live the unhappy life I did when I last came to England, I would stay abroad for ever. My mind is as fixed as fate." His release came on June 19th, 1801, when he sailed in a brig, so as not to deprive the Fleet of a larger vessel.

V

His services during the campaign had been rewarded with the title of Viscount, and Graves had got a K.B., but neither he nor his brothers in arms had been thanked by Parliament or the City, and no medals had been issued for what he considered his most difficult victory. Various excuses were suggested—the feelings of the part of Sir Hyde's Fleet not engaged in the action must be considered, also the feelings of Denmark, now an ally. He realised that there was disapproval of him in high places. He suspected St. Vincent, and Troubridge particularly, of doing all that they could to keep him from the company of Lady Hamilton. The struggle was well sustained. He spent a very happy leave at Burford Bridge, and at Shepperton, with a large party which included his sycophantic brother William and family, and the Hamiltons. But Britain was still at war.

When he found himself appointed to command the

defence flotilla on the south-east coast, he hoisted his flag in the *Unité* frigate at Sheerness, and astonished all by his activity. The anniversary of the Nile saw him at sea trying to get off Boulogne, but all he was able to do there was to show the French that they could not, with impunity, come outside their ports, and he was soon assured that wherever invasion was coming from, it was not Boulogne. On the night of August 15th-16th he attempted to bring away or burn the flotilla lying there. The French boats, many of them aground, were chained together, and as soon as they were boarded, such a heavy fire broke out from the shore that his boarding parties were forced to retire with heavy loss. He anchored in the Downs the same night, and himself chose lodgings in Deal for Captain Edward Parker and Lieutenant Frederick Langford, both of whom had been severely wounded. The Hamiltons, as before accompanying the William Nelsons, were coming to Deal for a holiday. On the day that they were due to arrive, he was summoned on a wild-goose chase to Flushing, but by the end of a singularly lovely September, the Peace which was to be dubbed by the old King the Experimental seemed settled upon. He escorted his guests over his flagship, to the Naval Hospital, to Dover and Walmer castles and Ramsgate. Lady Hamilton visited his two favourite wounded officers daily, sent to Piccadilly for a sofa for Langford, and when she had to return to London, left behind her chaise for his use. Langford had never looked back, but the death in agony of

Parker, which took place shortly after the Hamiltons had gone home, hit Nelson hard. He was observed to shed tears as a body which had represented to him hopes unfulfilled in his stepson was lowered into the earth at a funeral which he attended as chief mourner.

Mr. Pitt, calling on a wild October day, found him " in a cold frigate " half sea-sick and racked with toothache, convinced that " I should have got well long ago in a warm room, with a good fire and sincere friends." The Minister agreed that it did seem hard that he should be kept " thumping in the Downs, now it is all over." Troubridge wrote advising brisk walks and flannel next the skin. Nelson's formal application to be allowed to strike his flag was crossed by permission for ten days' leave. " What a set of beasts! "

He charged up the drive of Merton Place, Surrey, under a home-made triumphal arch, with dawn on October 23rd, 1801. What he always insisted on calling " The Farm " had been bought for him by Lady Hamilton a month and more past. Her regard for what she called her " regained reputation " was strict, and she had discouraged a suggestion that he should run down to see Merton at a date when Sir William would be absent. He accepted the fact that at Merton they would have to " live retired," but this did not prove necessary. The appearance of the Admiral at the village church accompanied by his little niece, Charlotte, who found the places in his prayer-book for a man who had lost his right arm and eye in the service of his country, was found reassuring by country neighbours. Many called, including the Vicar. All his family arrived to stay, even his aged father, and many old mess-mates. In the City his popularity was undimmed. " How are ye, my hearty? Glad to see ye back! " roared a butcher of Cheapside, as a carriage long since relieved of its horses rocked Nelson towards the Guildhall on Lord Mayor's Day. His chief anxiety during the months of the Experimental Peace was financial. A sheet achieved by him on the night of March 8th, 1803, ran as follows:

Lord Nelson's Income and Property

My Exchequer Pension for the Nile	£2,000	0	0
Navy Pension for the loss of one arm and one eye	923	0	0
Half-pay as Vice-Admiral ..	465	0	0
Interest of £1,000	30	0	0
	£3,418	0	0

Outgoings of Lord Nelson

To Lady Nelson	£1,800	0	0
Interest of money owing ..	500	0	0
Pension to my Brother's Widow	200	0	0
To assist in educating my Nephews	150	0	0
Expenditure	£2,650	0	0
Income	£3,418	0	0

The result seemed to be " For Lord Nelson, £768 per annum," and in a single week his bills at Merton had amounted to £117 8s. 2½d. A delightful summer holiday had cost £480 odd. His tour had taken him by Oxford (where he had received a Degree from the University and the Freedom of the City) to Sir William's Milford Haven estates. A return journey via Swansea, Monmouth, Hereford and Birmingham, where he had been the hero of many functions, had confirmed his belief that his country still loved him. He also discovered that although his actions in private life might be causing grave displeasure to what he bitterly called "my Lords and Masters," he was indispensable. If hostilities should recommence, he was going to get the Mediterranean command. He had always wanted that. As he cast up his accounts, in a reception room of the Hamiltons' Piccadilly House, another difficulty which might have proved serious was quietly solving itself. Sir William was dying, " going off, as an inch of candle." He passed away without a sigh or a struggle on an April morning, in the arms of his wife and with Nelson holding his hand. Enigmatic to the last, he had left " to my dearest friend, Lord Nelson, Duke of Brontë, a very small token of the great regard I have for his Lordship, the most virtuous, loyal, and truly brave character I have ever met with. God bless him and shame fall on those who do not say Amen." The legacy was a portrait of Emma as a Bacchante. Last year Sir William had been talking of " a *wise* and *well concerted separation*," but although his complaint had been " that the whole attention of my wife is given to Lord N.," he had been careful to add, " I well know the purity of Lord N.'s friendship for Emma and me," and expressed his belief that a separation would be " essentially detrimental to all parties."

Lady Hamilton had been left insufficiently provided for, but she had hopes of a pension from the Government. Meanwhile, she should live at Merton, " Lady Paramount of all the territories and waters," guardian of Nelson's home while the owner was at sea. He was leaving her £100 a month for housekeeping, and hoped much that she would soon have Horatia there to bear her company.

War was declared on May 16th, 1803, and he set off for Portsmouth at 4 a.m. two days later.

* 7 *

Mediterranean Command

GIBRALTAR HAD not heard of the war, and was surprised by the arrival of Lord Nelson, flying his flag in a frigate. His orders were to confer at Malta with Governor Ball, and taking Admiral Bickerton's squadron under his command, proceed off Toulon with all possible despatch. A last instruction, brought on board the *Victory* just before he sailed, had told him that he must make an offer of that first-rate to Admiral Cornwallis, off Brest. He had, therefore, after a vain search of twenty-four hours, changed into H.M.S. *Amphion* (32) and told Captain Sam Sutton that if he did not fall in with Cornwallis within the week he must take the *Victory* back to Plymouth for further orders. Malta, like Gibraltar, had heard nothing of the resumed war, and a thirty-six-hours' call at " this out of the way place " convinced him that it would never suit him as a base for operations against an enemy in Toulon. He came in sight of " *Dear* Naples, if it is what it was," with mixed feelings, and did not land. The presence of a British man-of-war in their bay, always ready to evacuate them,

would be a more tactful attention to their Majesties
at present than a personal call. The Queen was now
said to have three lovers, all French emigrés. He
had begun to fear that her failure to respond to his
mentions of Lady Hamilton's penurious widowhood
was deliberate. " If she can forget Emma, I hope
God will forget her." Maria-Carolina did forget, and
Nelson dismissed her from his calculations as " a time-
serving woman."

His duty now was to keep such a watch on the
French fleet as to ensure an engagement if it put to
sea. His force was certainly not superior in numbers.
All the ships which he took under his command had
been expecting to go home and were in need of dock-
ing repairs. They had fuel for one month, and having
been six months at sea, dependent upon Malta, no
provisions. Within a month of his arrival amongst
officers who were for the most part " perfect strangers,"
his letters were beginning to display a confident and
familiar ring. Every day, he hoped for his flagship.
She came in sight at last, on the morning of July 30th,
1803, and that evening her log recorded, " Joined this
ship, Captain T. M. Hardy, and superseded Captain
Sutton. Hoisted Lord Viscount Nelson's Flag." The
scene was now set, and many of the *dramatis personæ*
were assembled, for the final act; for although he had
two years and two months of life to run, he was to
spend but twenty-six nights out of H.M.S. *Victory*.

II

In the *Victory* he had three commodious rooms at his disposal, under the poop, immediately beneath those of Hardy. They consisted of state-room, " Great Cabin " or reception room, dining cabin and sleeping cabin, and taken with his gallery and steward's room, accounted for rather more than a quarter of the whole upper deck. This setting had been the background for the figures of Keppel, Kempenfelt, Howe, Hood and St. Vincent.

Dr. Gillespie, Physician to the Fleet, and Mr. William Beatty, Surgeon, wrote down impressions of Nelson in the *Victory*. The Admiral breakfasted at about quarter to seven, with Captains Murray and Hardy, his Chaplain, the Rev. Alexander Scott (who also acted as Admiral's Interpreter), his Secretary, young Mr. John Scott, and one or two other officers. Afterwards, even when it was blowing fresh, they went on deck to enjoy a majestic sunrise. H.M.S. *Victory*, " a floating city " mounting 110 guns and designed to carry water and provisions for four months and a ship's company of nine hundred, went through the Mediterranean with the greatest steadiness, followed in regular train by other " lofty and tremendous bulwarks of Britain." Unless other duties called, Lord Nelson and Dr. Scott met every morning to sit in two leathern arm-chairs, with large pockets stuffed with documents awaiting translation, and the interpreter was startled by his employer's ability to collect a few grains of intelligence from a bundle of apparent rubbish. " That man possessed the wisdom of the serpent with the innocence of the dove." Mr. John Scott found, " In my travels through the Service, I have met with no character in any degree equal to his Lordship; his penetration is quick, judgment clear, wisdom great, and his decisions correct and decided . . . Nor does he in company appear to bear any weight on his mind; so cheerful and happy, it is a happiness to be about his hand."

The Admiral's dinner was announced by a drum beating to the tune of " The Roast Beef of Old England," and after coffee and liqueurs the company walked the deck again while a band played. After tea, at seven, he sent for " my family," " to sit and talk." He partook sparingly of the good things at his table. A liver or wing of a fowl, with vegetables, and a small dish of macaroni, sometimes taken with a glass of champagne, formed his main meal, and after it he never exceeded four glasses of wine, all diluted by Bristol water. He was generally on deck six or seven hours in the day, and often at night, insufficiently attired in a light overcoat, a leather or flannel waistcoat and thin shoes. He chose shoes because he could kick them off without summoning Gaetano Spedilo (previously valet to Sir William Hamilton), and he would pace the canvas-covered, black-and-white diced decks of his quarters in his wringing-wet stocking feet until they were dry.

No suspicion that he had any private anxieties ever

reached his officers. " The rule he inculcated was
that every man became a bachelor after he passed
the Rock of Gibraltar, and he was not very tardy in
showing that he practised what he preached." Yet,
as " a most terrible long winter " wore out, his
anxiety for news from home gave him bad nights.
He bade Lady Hamilton, whom he hoped now past
all danger, " kiss dear Horatia for me, and the other.
Call him what you please, if a girl, Emma." Not
until the end of March did he learn that " you was
recovering, but that dear little Emma was no more!
and that Horatia had been so very ill. . . . It was
just at bedtime, and I had time to reflect, and thank
God for sparing you, and our dear Horatia."

For two years his only certain method of ensuring
that a letter reached Lady Hamilton unopened was to
see it go into the breast pocket of a Captain taking a
ship home for repairs. He was haunted by fears that
Horatia might be left unprovided for, " dependent
upon smiles and frowns." He wrote twice to ask that
a strong netting be placed round the strip of the river
Wandle running through the garden at Merton, " that
the little thing may not tumble in." On pitch black
nights he " whose soul is at Merton," could see the
English red-brick country house, almost as clearly as if
the nine windows of the aft-most wall of his state-room
had looked forth upon ornamental waters of Surrey
instead of " the stormy gulph of Lyons." He was far
from firm when he heard of over-spending at " the
Farm " (" Your purse, my dear Emma, will always

be empty "), but a suggestion that a family party should join him was quickly quashed. " Imagine what a cruise off Toulon is! Even in summer time we have a hard gale every week, and two days' heavy swell. It would kill you, and myself, to see you. Much less possible to have Charlotte, Horatia, etc., on board ship! And I who have given orders to carry no women to sea in the *Victory* to be the first to break them! " His Sicilian estate had proved a bitter disappointment. He had received no rent for three years and seemed to have poured a fortune into it. (" I *long* to be out of debt.")

He believed the three danger points in his command to be the Straits of Gibraltar, the heel of Italy and Toulon. His Fleet was soon hearty; he wished his ships were half as good. " They are what we call crazy. I know well enough that if I was to go into Malta, I should save the ships during this bad season, but if I am to watch the French, I must be at sea, and if at sea, must have bad weather." By October, 1803, he had found in the Maddalena Islands " a hole to put the Fleet in "—an open roadstead on a neutral coast to which he could run from time to time, to water and provision, while frigates kept watch on Toulon. He attacked monotony by changing his cruising ground continually, and in spite of " the same faces and almost the same conversation " day in and day out, variances in the Mediterranean Fleet were minor and rare. Nobody asked to be sent home; he had " Thank God! no Court-Martials. . . . The

Admiralty fills all vacancies except *death* and nobody will die." On St. George's Day, 1804, on a general promotion, he was gazetted Vice-Admiral of the White, the highest rank he was to hold, but communications with home were so bad that he did not receive his commission till July.

As the weather grew warmer, that summer, the French Admiral began to exercise his ships outside the harbour. " Monsieur La Touche came out with eight Sail-of-the-Line and six Frigates, cut a caper off Sepet, and went in again. I was off, with five Ships-of-the-Line, and brought to for his attack, although I did not believe that anything was meant serious." His irritation was great when he read in the Press an account sent by La Touche to Buonaparte of how, after a chase, Nelson had fled out of sight. " I keep his letter, and, by God, if I take him he shall eat it." But in August La Touche died, according to the *Moniteur*, from sheer exhaustion, after walking so often to the Sepet signal post to watch for the British Fleet. (" I always pronounced that would be his death.")

The plans of Buonaparte did not at present include action in the Mediterranean. He was preparing for the invasion of England. He had assumed the Imperial purple, and on the Boulogne heights, his Grande Armée only awaited the order to sail. Nelson himself never really believed in the invasion, but he disapproved when he heard that Horatia was being taken to Canterbury, to stay with the William Nelsons.

" For on any alarm you must stay there, and in a town filled with soldiers." He wished that the child could be permanently at the farm, " fixed." Why not? But Lady Hamilton would not have her at Merton, except for short visits, and although complaining of the enormous cost of living, kept on a small house in Clarges Street.

Seventeen days of blowing weather in July decided Nelson that he had better not attempt another winter at sea. He was wearing a green shade, nevertheless his " good " eye was troubling him. His " letters relative to my health " were no sooner despatched than he regretted them, and the result was unfortunate. Bickerton was, as he had hoped, appointed to fill his place temporarily, but the station was sub-divided. Sir John Orde was sent with five of-the-line to blockade Cadiz. In view of war with Spain again, this was the station for prize-money. " He is sent off Cadiz to reap the golden harvest as Campbell was . . . to reap my sugar harvest. It's very odd, two Admiralties to treat me so; surely I have dreamt that ' I have done the State some Service.' " He kept his permission to go on leave in his pocket and took the Fleet to reconnoitre Toulon, where the French were said to be embarking troops. After a week of watching them still in port, he went to Maddalena. It was there, on the afternoon of January 19th, 1805, that his look-out frigates, H.M.S. *Active* and *Seahorse*, came in sight under a press of sail, flying the long-hoped-for signal, " The Enemy is at Sea."

III

Buonaparte had resolved to make an effort to gain command of the Channel. He had twenty ships in Brest, ten in Toulon and five in Rochefort, to which he was soon to add fifteen Spaniards. All were ordered to evade the British blockading squadrons, and avoiding action, hasten to the great French arsenal of Martinique. They were to proceed independently to deal havoc to British possessions in that quarter, and then unite for a dash back across the Atlantic and an unexpected appearance in the English Channel. He reckoned that at least thirty ships-of-the-line must be sent after them, and that while the Channel Fleet was overpowered or held in check, an army corps might be landed in Ireland and his main body on the English coast.

The fleet from Rochefort got out, but that from Toulon was shattered by a violent gale and returned to port. Nelson searched for it in a fever, for a month. When he learnt the truth, at Malta, he could only hope that their Lordships would approve of his having gone to the Morea and Egypt. He got his first pleasant surprise for many months on March 26th, when a frigate which saluted the *Victory* with thirteen guns at dinner hour proved to have brought him as replacement for George Campbell (one of his junior Admirals who was suffering from a nervous breakdown), an old friend, in whom he could put perfect reliance—Louis, who had commanded the *Minotaur* at the Nile. But at 10 p.m., five days after he had congratulated himself on the prospect of a little rest, history repeated itself. The faithful *Phoebe* had seen the last of the Toulon Fleet with sunset on March 31st, steering S.S.W. with a light breeze at N.E. and all sails set. The Long Chase had begun.

It opened for Nelson by his being without news of the enemy for twelve days. As in January, he had to weigh all the possibilities of Naples, Sicily, Sardinia, the Morea and Egypt. He covered the channel from Barbary to Tunis, and took up a stationary position between Sardinia and Galita. On April 9th, he started back from Palermo to Toulon. He had beaten against a head wind for a week when he heard the startling rumour that the French Fleet had passed the Rock, and he could not get a fair wind, or even a side-wind. "Dead foul! Dead foul!" He guessed, from the fact that Spanish ships from Cadiz had joined Admiral Villeneuve, that their destination might be Brest or Ireland. It was not until May 4th that he reached Mazari Bay on the African coast, where, as he could not pass the Gut, he anchored to water. Here he was joined by a frigate from Gibraltar, after which he confided to Admiral Keats, "I am like to have a West India trip." Next day he was able to get across to Rosia Bay, to provision. That his decision to go to the Antilles had hardened after a private call from Real-Admiral Donald Campbell of the Portuguese naval service was never mentioned by him, but

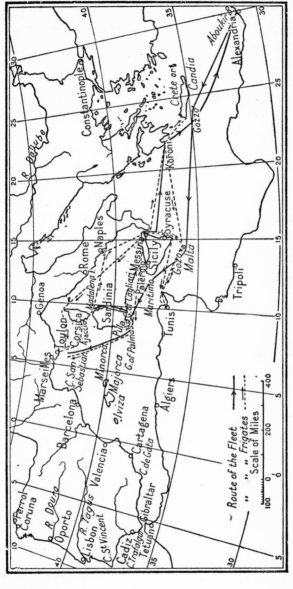

NELSON'S SEARCH IN THE MEDITERRANEAN

within four months, at the instigation of the French
Ambassador at Lisbon, Campbell, an officer in the
service of a neutral power, lost his command.

By 7 p.m. on the night of May 11th, Nelson's fleet,
provisioned for a five months' cruise, was under full
sail for the Antilles. He hoped, by " exertion," to
gain a fortnight on an enemy whom he now believed
to be set on capturing the Jamaicas. The *Superb*,
overdue for repairs, was still with him. Richard Keats,
" that treasure of the Service," asked for permission
not to stop when the other ships did, and lashed his
studdings sails to his yards. Nelson sent him a typical
line. " I know and feel that the *Superb* does all which
is possible for a Ship to accomplish; and I desire you
will not fret upon the occasion." But he could not
help fretting himself. " Half killed " by anxiety, he
wrote to Davison, " I know it cannot last long, what
I feel." His home mail had gone up the Mediterranean, and " will never be received by me . . . but
salt beef and the French Fleet is far preferable to
roast beef and champagne without them." He had
entirely put behind him the dream of leave at Merton,
in a house which Lady Hamilton knew how to make
welcoming. The phrase " Self is out of the question "
first began to appear in his letters as he toiled past
Madeira, in very fine weather and " going with a
soft wind." While the Fleet was standing into the
Trades, he transmitted to his Captains his provisional
plans for attack at sea. On May 27th he calculated,
" We shall be at Barbados the 3rd or 4th June. . . .

Our passage, although not very quick, has been far from a bad one." He anchored in Carlisle Bay on the 4th, and Admiral Cochrane and General Sir William Myers came on board to tell him something disconcerting. A letter from General Brereton, received yesterday from St. Lucia, said that an allied fleet of twenty-eight sail had passed Gros Islet going south, during the night of May 28th-29th. Against his instinct and inclination, Nelson sailed south for Trinidad. Afterwards he mourned, " If either General Brereton could not have wrote, or his look-out man had been blind, nothing could have prevented my fighting them on June 6th."

That he had been acting on incorrect information, and had missed his battle, was made clear to him by the Governor of Dominica and confirmed by General Prevost, who had actually seen an enemy fleet of eighteen of-the-line under the Saints standing to the northward on the night of June 6th. This report, which could not be doubted, made him guess the truth—that Villeneuve had fled, not from the face, but from the very name of Nelson, and was " pushing for Europe to get out of our way."

After having ascertained that all was well at Antigua and St. Kitts, Nelson prepared to re-cross the Atlantic in haste. " I flew to the West Indies without any orders, but I think the Ministry cannot be displeased." He had saved the Colonies and upwards of two hundred sugar-laden ships, and he still did not despair of matching his eleven men-of-war against eighteen (twenty was his own belief) if he could get up with the enemy before they reached the shelter of Cadiz or Toulon. Villeneuve had only five days' start of him this time. On the 22nd he retired from his quarter-deck to write in his private diary, " Midnight, nearly calm. Saw three planks, which I think came from the French Fleet. Very miserable, which is very foolish." One of his Captains was writing home mean-while, " We are all half-starved, and otherwise incon-venienced by being so long away from a port, but our full recompense is that we are with Nelson."

By the last day of the month he had sent away his last frigate, to discover if the enemy had entered the Mediterranean. Sutton, given a rendezvous off Cape Spartel, was told to keep the approach of Nelson as secret as possible, and to rouse about the British Consul at Tangier so that bullocks, onions, lemons and oranges, in large numbers, might be ready for his arrival. His Fleet was crawling now—" only thirty-three miles in twenty-four hours." His hope was that Villeneuve was near him and in the same situation.

In fact, the meeting for which he was longing had fallen to another Admiral. The *Curieux* brig, despatched on June 12th, had sighted the enemy 900 miles N.N.E. of St. John, Antigua, and kept company long enough to ascertain numbers and course. Her Captain was in the presence of the First Lord before breakfast on July 9th. Within a few hours, despatch vessels were under sail with orders for the blockading squadrons off Rochefort and Ferrol. Sir Robert Calder's squadron

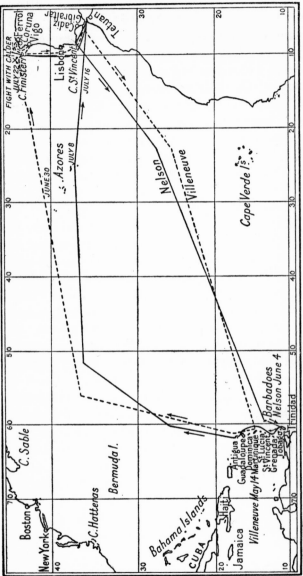

THE CHASE TO THE WEST INDIES

Villeneuve passed Str. of Gibraltar April 9   Villeneuve left Antigua June 8
Nelson passed Str. of Gibraltar May 10   Nelson left Antigua June 13

of fifteen of-the-line met Villeneuve 100 miles west of Cape Finisterre on the cloudy morning of July 22nd. The action, which took place at long range, was indecisive, and Calder joined Cornwallis west of Ushant one day before Nelson, who, delayed by northerly winds, had been three weeks making his passage from the Rock to the Channel Fleet. He had set down in his diary on the night of July 20th:

"I went on shore for the first time since the 16th of June, 1803; and from having my foot out of the *Victory* two years, wanting ten days."

The *Victory* saluted Admiral Cornwallis's flagship and hove to, but was soon under sail again. Cornwallis had excused Nelson even the customary personal visit, and authorised him to go on to Portsmouth. His order of release from quarantine ("for the first time in my life") came on the night of August 19th. In an express he had told Lady Hamilton, from whom he had not heard since April, "I have brought home no honour for my Country . . . nor any riches—that the Administration took care to give to others—but I have brought home a most faithful and honourable heart . . . God send us a happy meeting as our parting was sorrowful."

* 8 *
Trafalgar

THE GENERALLY accepted picture of Nelson basking in heat-wave peace at Merton, alone with Lady Hamilton, during his last weeks in England, is mistaken. He was in London for at least part of fourteen of the famous twenty-five days of broken weather, and within nine had heard from Pitt that his services might be wanted. Moreover, Lady Hamilton provided a crowd-scene of perpetually changing guests.

Lord Minto took his chance one day, and found the Admiral "just sitting down to dinner surrounded by a family party" at a festal board ornamented by Worcester porcelain decorated with oak-leaves and laurel, and the coat of arms of Viscount Nelson, Duke of Brontë. There were several young people present, and the guest took Horatia, now four and a half years old and "uncommonly quick," for one of "the children of a sister." He disapproved of the interior decoration of the hero's home. The place was a perfect Nelson and Emma Museum. Even the staircase walls were covered by "pictures of her and him, of all sizes and sorts, and representations of his naval actions."

Of Lady Hamilton, however, he took a more indulgent view than previously. He thought the new dining-room, built apparently during the owner's absence, and without his knowledge, a great improvement. " She is a clever being after all; the passion is as hot as ever." As a new drawing-room also had been ordered, one of Nelson's calls at a silversmith's shop that week was in order to dispose of some of his presentation plate.

" The public appearance in the streets of Lord Nelson, who in the short space of five weeks has viewed the four quarters of the Globe, attracted a concourse." The twenty-five days are well documented. When obliged to stay the night in town, Gordon's Hotel, Albemarle Street, was his address. He was observed arriving at the Admiralty, and Downing Street, and at The Ship, Greenwich. He was mobbed in Piccadilly. He was thought to be looking remarkably well, and in good spirits, wearing " plain uniform and a green shade over his left eye," his cocked hat " put on square and much lower than the others." At Merton he appeared in a simple suit of black. Here he paced the walk designed to remind him of his quarter-deck, and explained his Plan for Attack to Captain Keats. He always took an early turn in his garden, so when Captain Blackwood arrived at 5 a.m. on the morning of September 1st, he was greeted with the words, " I am sure that you bring me news of the French and Spanish Fleets, and that I shall have to beat them yet."

Five days later Lord Nelson's new command was announced, and his heavy luggage was put on the road for Portsmouth. His old mess-mate, Prince William Henry, attended the christening of a Suckling god-child at Merton that day. In the morning, at Downing Street, while a heavy thunderstorm shook London, the Admiral had told Ministers with boyish eagerness, that he wanted to do " the job " well. " It is, as Mr. Pitt knows, annihilation that the Country wants, and not merely a splendid victory of twenty-three to thirty-six, honourable to the parties concerned, but absolutely useless in the extended scale, to bring Buonaparte to his marrow-bones."

Friday, September 13th, was to be his last day at home. He had hoped to spend Thursday in peace, but Lords Castlereagh and Mulgrave needed to see him, and the Prince of Wales had come up to town from Weymouth specially. After his call at Carlton House, Nelson went on to the Colonial Office. It was in the little waiting-room on the right of the hall that he met for the first and only time in his life General the Hon. Sir Arthur Wellesley. The Victor of Assaye instantly recognised the Victor of the Nile, " from his likeness to his pictures, and the loss of an arm. . . . He entered into conversation with me, if I can call it conversation, for it was almost all on his side, and all about himself, and in, really, a style so vain and silly as to surprise and almost disgust me." Sir Arthur was not too disgusted to remark on Sir Robert Calder's recent action, " Your Lordship has taught the public to expect something more brilliant," and he was amused that the Admiral almost at once left the room, evidently to inquire as to the identity of the curt, high-nosed military officer who embodied all that he found unsympathetic in the junior Service. " When he came back, he was altogether a different man, both in manner and matter. . . . He talked like an officer and a statesman. The Secretary of State kept us long waiting, and certainly, for the last half or three quarters of an hour, I don't know that I ever had a conversation that interested me more . . . He really was a very superior man."

At Merton, a dinner-party waited, unintroduced to one another, for two hours. When at last the master of the house arrived, his geniality turned the scales in favour of a pleasant evening, but tragedy entered in the person of Lady Hamilton. From her appearance it was plain that the last drive together had just taken place. All Lord Minto's old aversion returned as he occupied the seat of honour next to a hostess who could not restrain large tears, " could not eat, and hardly drink, and near swooning, and all at table."

The post-chaise which was to carry the Admiral through the night to Portsmouth drew up outside the doors of Merton after dinner next day. His sister, Kitty Matcham, and her husband, stayed in the drawing-room when he went upstairs for the last time. In Horatia's bedroom he dropped on his knees and prayed that the life of the sleeping child might be happy. That prayer was answered. Horatia married an amiable though impecunious clergyman, and bore many children. But when she was laid to rest in Pinner churchyard, an octogenarian, the inscription on her tombstone claimed no more than that she had been the adopted daughter of Lord Nelson. She never knew her parentage. She hoped that Nelson had been her father, and would never believe that Lady Hamilton could have been her mother. . . .

Nelson came downstairs alone, speaking cheerfully. He voiced regrets that he had not been able to repay a sum of £4,000 borrowed from his wealthy brother-in-law. Matcham replied with difficulty, " My dear Lord, I have no other wish than to see you return home in safety."

A prayer which Nelson entered in his private diary, later that night, while horses were being changed, was copied by the Rev. Alexander Scott:

" Friday night, at half-past ten, drove from dear, dear Merton, where I left all which I hold dear in this world, to go to serve my king and country. May the great God whom I adore, enable me to fulfill the expectations of my country; and if it is His good pleasure that I should return, my thanks will never cease being offered up to the throne of His mercy. If it is His good Providence to cut short my days upon earth, I bow with the greatest submission, relying that He will protect those so dear to me, that I may leave behind. His will be done. Amen, Amen, Amen."

II

His departure from Portsmouth was an extraordinary scene. As the town was very full on a Saturday afternoon, and a mob had gathered outside the George, he decided to embark from the beach at Southsea, and left the inn by a back entrance. He was quickly discovered, and had to push his way through a pressing multitude. He did this in good vein, explaining that he was sorry that as he had not two arms, he could not shake hands with more friends. As his figure came in sight, some people dropped to their knees in silence, and uncovered; others called out a blessing on him; many wept. He turned to Hardy, in his barge, after they had pushed off, and as the regular dip of oars gained pre-eminence over Portsmouth cheers on an afternoon of flat calm, he said, " I had their huzaas before. I have their hearts now."

The almost solitary progress of the *Victory* towards Cape Trafalgar was stately in pace. Not until September 25th did he send home a letter opening, " My dearest Emma,—We are now in sight of the Rock of Lisbon, and although we have very little wind, I hope to get round Cape St. Vincent to-morrow. . . . I am anxious to join the Fleet, for it would add to my grief if any other man was to give them the Nelson touch, which WE say is warranted never to fail."

Dawn of the 28th disclosed a British bomb-ketch cruising. By noon he could see eighteen of-the-line. With warm dusk that night he " got fairly into the Fleet," stationed between fifteen and twenty miles from Cadiz, and getting short of water and provisions.

The rule of Collingwood had been severe. Officers who had never seen the Victor of the Nile had been praying, " For Charity's sake, send us Lord Nelson, ye men of power! " He had sent word that the enemy must not know of his approach. " I would not have you salute even if you are out of sight of land." He had been enthusiastically greeted before, when taking over a command, but on this occasion even he was surprised by the warmth of his welcome. The omission of salutes and hoisting of colours, at a moment when a Fleet action was hourly expected, was realised by all as dramatic. Lord Nelson had arrived silently. It was his birthday. He was forty-seven.

> " The reception I met with on joining the Fleet caused the sweetest sensation of my life. The Officers who came on board to welcome my return, forgot my rank as Commander-in-Chief in the enthusiasm with which they greeted me. As soon as these emotions were past, I laid before them the Plan I had previously arranged for attacking the Enemy; and it was not only my pleasure to find it generally approved, but clearly perceived and understood."

Lady Hamilton was told, on October 1st: " When I came to explain to them the ' Nelson touch,' it was

like an electric shock." His previous use of the phrase
had suggested that the " Nelson touch " was something personal; the impact of his individuality. But
this time the context shows that it was something
concrete—his Plan of Attack. " It was new—it was
singular—it was simple! " From Admirals down, all
officers repeated, " It must succeed if ever they will
allow us to get at them! " A week later, he issued
formally, in a secret memorandum, the Plan of Attack,
in which are to be found the essential ideas eventually
adapted to suit the conditions at Trafalgar.

By that date all the enemy men-of-war in Cadiz
harbour, save one, had moved out of the Puerto Real.
He had hoped for this result when he had moved his
own Fleet fifty miles west of the port. He trusted that
the enemy were still in ignorance how he was rein-
forced. He ordered Louis to take six ships to Gibraltar
and Tetuan, to water and re-provision. An old
" Crocodile," (Captain of the Nile), was reproachful.
" You are sending us away, my Lord—the Enemy
will come out, and we shall have no share in the
Battle." " I send you first, to insure your being here
to help to beat them." But Louis was right.

A squadron of frigates keeping watch on the harbour's mouth reported, " Enemy getting their troops
on board," " Enemy out of port, top-gallant sails
bent." A notification of Louis's arrival at Gibraltar,
and the news that his successor had reached Madrid,
had goaded Villeneuve into putting to sea. He had
under his command fifteen Spaniards of-the-line, four

Plate 5 Lord Nelson. Oil sketch by Sir William Beechey

Plate 6 The Battle of Trafalgar by Nicholas Pocock

Plate 7 The Death of Nelson by Arthur W. Devis

of them three-deckers, four French 80-gun ships and fourteen 74s, five frigates and two gun-brigs, all French. Of Nelson's twenty-seven ships when he came to action, seven were three-deckers, one was an 80-gun ship, sixteen were 74s and three 64s. A week before the battle he had deprived himself of a three-decker in order to allow Sir Robert Calder, whom he had been told to send home for court martial in a frigate, to depart in his own ship. " He is in adversity."

On the night of the 16th, as he toiled through the dictation of letters, heavy rain began to fall, to the irritation of officers who had almost completed re-painting their ships *à la Nelson*—in imitation of the *Victory*, with black bands between the varnish-yellow of the gun-decks, and black ports, so that, with closed ports, the ship presented a chequered appearance. Five more of-the-line had now joined him from home, and one from the Rock. When the *Agamemnon* was signalled, he rubbed his " fin " and smiled. " Here comes Berry! Now we shall have a battle."

The combined Fleets of France and Spain began to get under way at 7 a.m. on the 19th, but from want of wind only twelve ships effected their exit that day. During the afternoon, a favourable breeze sprang up, and they stood on the larboard tack to the northward, dogged by two of Nelson's frigates. During the interval, before the news raced from masthead to masthead, " The Enemy's Fleet is at sea," he had retired to his cabin to write two personal letters. The first opened, " My Dearest beloved Emma, the dear friend of my bosom," the second, addressed to " My dearest Angel," was signed simply " Your Father."

III

Daylight of October 20th found the British Fleet close to the mouth of the Straits, in heavy rain and thick weather. Through the sea-fret could be seen, upon the eastern horizon, the towering cliffs of Cape Trafalgar. He wrote in his diary, " The Enemy appear determined to push to the westward. That they shall not do, if in the power of Nelson and Brontë to prevent them."

A little before dawn on the 21st, he ordered his Fleet, hitherto sailing almost parallel to the enemy, though out of sight, to alter course. He had drawn Villeneuve far enough out of Cadiz, and had turned to the N.E. as a preliminary to attack. Throughout the night there had been light breezes inclining to calm, but the heavy swell from the westward might herald a storm.

He was observed on the quarter-deck of the *Victory* with first light, wearing an undress uniform coat. It was well worn, but its left breast exhibited embroidered stars of the four Orders of Knighthood to which he was entitled. The enemy were believed to have Tyrolean riflemen in their ships, and were likely to have sharpshooters in their tops. Beatty, and both the Scotts, wished that somebody would draw the Admiral's attention to this fact, but it fell to Hardy to suggest something bound to result in a reproof.

Nelson agreed that his decorations might draw enemy attention to his figure, but said " it was now too late to be shifting a coat."

The *Victory's* first general signal of the day, to form the order of sailing in two columns, each ship to engage her opponent, was followed after ten minutes by " Bear up, and steer east." The Commander-in-Chief, leading the twelve ships of the weather column, set the example, and Collingwood's leeward division of fifteen ships fell into the wake of his flagship. One of the frigate Captains who had come on board the *Victory* was asked before he departed to witness the document always described as Nelson's " last Codicil " though that word nowhere occurs in it. Captains Hardy and Blackwood set their names to a sheet of four paragraphs, repeating the catalogue of Lady Hamilton's national services.

> " I leave Emma, Lady Hamilton, therefore, as legacy to my King and Country. . . . I leave to the beneficence of my Country my adopted daughter. . . . These are the only favours I ask of my King and Country at this moment when I am going to fight their Battle."

The approach to action was at a rate which promised a heavy casualty list for the leading ships, for the British advance, though with all possible sail set, fell from three knots to a mile and a half an hour. A little before eleven, Nelson went down to his cabin for the last time. His last entry in his pocket-book was a prayer for a great and glorious victory. John Pasco, Signal Lieutenant, entering with a report, found him on his knees.

"Mr. Pasco," he said, when they had reached the poop, "I wish you to say to the Fleet ENGLAND CONFIDES THAT EVERY MAN WILL DO HIS DUTY. You must be quick, for I have one more signal to make, which is for close action." Pasco begged leave to suggest that "expects" for "confides" would save seven hoists, and was told, "That will do; make it directly." The response through the Fleet was "truly sublime." The signal was received in every ship with three cheers, and "Number 16," which followed, remained at the top-gallant masthead of the *Victory* until it was shot away. It had been preceded by four minutes by the order to be prepared to anchor after action. The sea was smooth, and under cloudless skies, a rich dark blue in colour. But the great ground-swell setting from the westward had been considered by Nelson. In view of storm, he was anxious for the safety of his ships on a lee shore.

Bands struck up on board the ships of the two British columns rolling gently towards the enemy, and sunlight, breaking through, picked up a forest of masts with black hoops and the freshly painted sides of a crescent-shaped formation of scarlet, black and yellow French and Spanish men-of-war. Nelson struck his thigh and exclaimed, "See how that noble fellow Collingwood carries his ship into action!" These were the last words spoken by him without the accom-

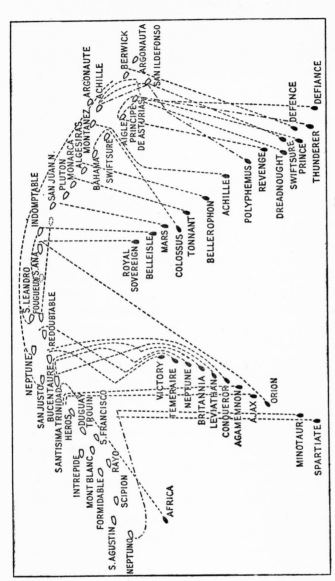

THE ATTACK AT TRAFALGAR ABOUT NOON

paniment of gun-fire, for by 11.40 Collingwood had broken the line astern of the Spanish three-decker bearing the flag of Vice-Admiral de Álava.

The first shot at the *Victory* fell short of her. She was an almost stationary target, carried along by the long Atlantic swell, and the remains of her own impetus. A second shot fell alongside, and a third passed over her. The frigate Captains went over her side, with orders to tell the Captains of all line-of-battle ships to get into action immediately. (Blackwood was shocked by Nelson's farewell. " God bless you. I shall never speak to you again.") The enemy found the range of the *Victory* with their sixth shot, and after a short silence, seven or eight of their van poured in broadsides. A round shot, flying across the quarter-deck, almost tore in two the figure of Admiral Nelson's Secretary, in the act of speech with Hardy. The fragmentary corpse was cast overboard without delay, but Nelson had noticed. " Is that poor Scott? "

As firing became general, the scene became enveloped by smoke. The *Victory* held steadily on to her course. Her mizzen-top mast was shot away about two-thirds up; her sails were soon riddled. The French were following their practice of concentrating on masts and rigging. Her most serious loss came when her wheel was knocked to pieces. But the tiller was quickly manned, and she was thereafter steered from the gun-room. A shot penetrating the thickness of four hammocks in the nettings, hit the forebrace bitts on the quarter-deck. Nelson and his Flag-Captain halted and looked one another up and down, but the only casualty was the buckle of Hardy's left shoe. The Admiral said with a smile, " This is too warm work to last long," and resumed his walk.

After about twenty minutes of receiving punishment without the possibility of reply, the *Victory* opened fire " in a determined, cool and steady manner." The first-rate into which she delivered her first fatal counter-stroke was Villeneuve's flagship. Acrid smoke puffed back into the *Victory's* gun-ports, filling her lower decks, and a cloud of black dust and shower of splinters descended on the quarter-deck. But close behind the *Bucentaure* lay the French 80-gun *Neptune*, and astern of her a 74 in the act of ranging up. Hardy, told, " It does not signify which we run on board of," chose the 74. After the collision the *Victory's* yard-arm caught in the rigging of the French *Redoubtable*, and the two ships, locked in a death-grip, moved slowly before the wind to the S.S.E.

The mizzen-mast of the smaller ship rose midway between the *Victory's* mizzen and main, and the crouching riflemen, rising breast-high to fire, had the English Commander-in-Chief's quarter-deck not forty-five feet distant and immediately below them. About 1.35 Hardy, who had turned at the wheel, and was advancing towards the hatchway, realised that he was walking alone. Facing about, he saw the Admiral on his knees, with the fingertips of his left hand just touching the deck. The single arm gave way, and he fell on his left side. As Hardy bent he saw a smile and heard the words, " Hardy, I believe they have done it at last."

IV

On the arrival of one more shuffling party into a cockpit which was " like a butcher's shambles," Surgeon Beatty ordered it far forward on the port side. He heard a murmur, " Lord Nelson is here," and turning, saw a handkerchief fall from a pale countenance, and a coat with stars upon its breast.

The easy business of stripping a one-armed man was quickly performed. Next to his skin the Admiral had been wearing a large miniature set as a locket. Its picture was of Lady Hamilton, high-coloured and smiling—a Bacchante. Almost his first words after he opened his eyes were of her—a repetition of his statement that he left her and his adopted daughter as a legacy to his country. Beatty soon satisfied himself that a ball had gone deep into the chest, and probably lodged in the spine. Nelson said, " I felt it break my back." The cockpit, in which three surgeons and their mates were working with reddened forearms by the light of candles in swaying horn lanterns, was below the water-line. Beatty suggested to Dr. Scott, who was wringing his hands, the construction of a paper fan, and the administration of sips of lemonade.

Once, as the minutes dragged past, the dreadful cry of " Fire " penetrated. From time to time the sound of British cheers swelled. It was nearly three o'clock when the comfortable figure of Hardy came stooping towards the midshipman's berth in which the Admiral had been laid. An historic dialogue was recorded by Surgeon Beatty.

" Well, Hardy, how goes the battle? How goes the day with us? "

" Very well, my Lord. We have got twelve or fourteen of the enemy's Ships in our possession, but five of their van have tacked, and show an intention of bearing down upon the *Victory*. I have, therefore, called two or three of our fresh ships round us, and have no doubt of giving them a drubbing."

" I hope none of *our* ships have struck, Hardy? "

" No, my Lord. There is no fear of that."

" I am a dead man, Hardy. I am going fast; it will be all over with me soon. . . ."

The purser, who together with Scott had been supporting him in a semi-recumbent position, perceived that something very intimate was to be disclosed. He made to remove his arm from behind the pillow but was desired not to move, so heard the low-spoken message. " Pray let dear Lady Hamilton have my hair, and all other things belonging to me." The Chief Surgeon, who had been performing an amputation, approached, and Hardy voiced hearty hopes of " some prospect of life." " Oh no," whispered the patient. " Beatty will tell you. My back is shot through." Beatty kept silence, and Hardy departed to send a warning of the impending tragedy to Collingwood.

His second call lasted not more than eight minutes. As before, a formal handshake opened the dialogue, but this time Hardy kept his hand in that of Nelson as he announced that he was come to congratulate him, even in the arms of death, " on a brilliant victory, which is complete." He could answer for fourteen or fifteen ships. The reply was, " That is well, but I had bargained for twenty," and then with an access of energy, the order " *Anchor*, Hardy, *anchor*."

The suggestion that his Second should now take upon himself the direction of affairs brought Nelson almost upright in the arms of his attendants. " Not while I live, I hope! " But he believed that he had only a few minutes left. He mentioned, " Don't throw me overboard, Hardy." " Oh, no, certainly not! " was the wretched answer. Beatty wrote down all that followed.

" Then," replied his Lordship, " you know what to do. And take care of poor Lady Hamilton. Kiss me, Hardy."

The Captain knelt down and kissed his cheek, when his Lordship said, " Now I am satisfied; thank God I have done my duty."

Captain Hardy stood a minute or two, in silent contemplation. He knelt down again, and kissed his Lordship's forehead.

His Lordship said, " Who is that? "

The Captain answered, " It is Hardy," to which his Lordship replied, " God bless you, Hardy! "

After Hardy's second withdrawal, the patient articulated with growing difficulty requests for " Fan —fan," or " Rub—rub." The *Victory* had ceased to fire some time past, and within the next few minutes the last gun-fire of the greatest naval victory in history died away. He whispered, " I wish I had not left the deck," and presently, to Scott, " I have not been a great sinner, doctor," followed by " *Remember* that I leave Lady Hamilton and my daughter as a legacy to my Country—never forget Horatia."

Beatty, returning frequently, found him repeating in fainter and fainter tones, " Thank God, I have done my duty." About three hours after he had been hit, his lips ceased to move. His Neapolitan steward gesticulated meaningly, and Beatty hurried up. They had to touch the shoulder of the Chaplain, who was still mechanically chafing a cold breast in which the heart no longer beat.

T H E   E N D

Chronological Table

1758 Birth of Nelson.
1770 Entered the Navy.
1773 North Pole Expedition.
1776 Invalided home from East Indies.
1777 Lieutenant.
1779 Post-Captain.
1780 San Juan Expedition. Invalided home. Half-pay.
1782 First meeting with Lord Hood, off New York.
1783 Half-pay. Visited France during Peace.
1784–1787 In West Indies. Married Mrs. Nisbet.
1787–1793 " On the Beach."
1793 War with France resumed. " Old Mediterranean Man."
    First meeting with Lady Hamilton.
1794 Lost right eye at siege of Calvi.
1795 Commodore.
1797 Battle of Cape St. Vincent. Promoted Rear-Admiral of
    the Blue, and appointed K.B. Lost right arm in attack
    on Santa Cruz.
1798 Battle of the Nile. Wounded. Created Baron and
    promoted Rear-Admiral of the Red.
1798–1800 In Mediterranean, principally at Naples and
    Palermo. Duke of Brontë. Struck his flag and re-
    turned home.
1801 Vice-Admiral of the Blue. Birth of Horatia. Separated
    from Lady Nelson. Battle of Copenhagen. Created
    Viscount. In command of squadron for Home Defence.
    Peace with France. Bought Merton.
1803 Death of Sir William Hamilton. War with France re-
    sumed. Nelson appointed Commander-in-Chief, Medi-
    terranean. Flag in H.M.S. *Victory.*
1804 Vice-Admiral of the White.
1805 The Long Chase. " Twenty-Five Days' " leave. Trafalgar.

A Note on Sources

FIVE YEARS after the death of Nelson, the Rev. James Clarke, and John M'Arthur, both of whom had been afloat in the Royal Service, produced a two-volume biography, containing much material supplied by his family. This semi-official publication had no index, and did not pretend to deal with the hero's private life after the Battle of the Nile. The Poet Laureate, in 1813, added scarcely any information, and some mistakes, but " Southey's Nelson " is a literary classic.

The seven-volume collection of *The Letters and Despatches of Vice-Admiral Lord Viscount Nelson*, completed in 1846 by Sir Harris Nicolas, remains to-day the Bible of the Nelson student. Nicolas had access to the ninety-two volumes of MS. inherited by Nelson's niece, Charlotte. This collection was bought by the British Museum in 1895 and is catalogued as Add. MSS. 34,902-92 & 35,191. Another collection, privately printed in 1894, and generally known as *The Morrison MS.*, has since been dispersed, but is an essential source. It contains hundreds of letters from Nelson to Lady Hamilton. Fifty-five letters missing from this collection came to light in 1949, amongst the papers of Sir Thomas Phillipps (1792-1872), and are now in the possession of the National Maritime Museum, Greenwich, where also are to be found the Nelson Ward MSS., which represent the property of Nelson's daughter, Horatia. In 1958 *Nelson's Letters to his wife and other Documents, 1785-1831*, edited by G. P. B. Naish, were published in conjunction with the Navy Records Society by Routledge & Kegan Paul.

The Nelson Museum, Monmouth, contains five bound volumes of holograph correspondence, from the pens of Nelson and his family, four portfolios, formerly the property of Lady Nelson, and five Nelson " Letter Books " (official correspondence) and five logs. Comparison of the first three volumes of " Nelson Papers " in the Monmouth collection with the publication by Clarke and M'Arthur is interesting. All the letters quoted by them are here, but they not only cut, and ran several letters into one; they altered the wording, giving false evidence repeated by every succeeding Nelson biographer.

Acknowledgments

The author wishes to thank Messrs. Hodder & Stoughton for permission to draw upon the material and research contained in her full-length biography of *Nelson*, published, 1947.

The Illustrations

Frontispiece. Lord Nelson by John Hoppner. Nelson, aged 43, gave sittings for this portrait before March 1802. An engraving by Meyer was published 1805 and an enamel by Bone was exhibited at the Royal Academy in the same year. The naval engagement in the background of this version is Copenhagen but in engravings published after Nelson's death Trafalgar was substituted.

From the Royal Collection at St. James's Palace; reproduced by gracious permission of Her Majesty the Queen.

Plate 1. Lady Nelson by Daniel Orme. A water-colour miniature taken in 1798 when she was about forty.
By permission of the National Maritime Museum.

Plate 2 Lady Hamilton as a bacchante by Henry Bone. This miniature, after a painting by Vigée le Brun, was left by Sir William Hamilton to Nelson in his will.
By permission of the Wallace Collection.

Plates 3 and 4. Lord Nelson and Lady Hamilton by J. H. Schmidt. Schmidt, Court Painter to the King of Saxony, made sketches for these pastels at the Hôtel de Pologne, Dresden, in October 1800. The portrait of Lady Hamilton shows her wearing her decoration as *Dame Petite Croix* of the order of St. John of Jerusalem. This was awarded by the Czar, as Grand Master, for her exertions in obtaining supplies for the Maltese when besieged. Nelson showed the picture in his cabin at Rostock to the Duke of Mecklenburg-Strelitz, after the Copenhagen victory. It had been " in the battle."

By permission of the Maritime Museum.

Plate 5. Lord Nelson by Sir William Beechey. A sketch in oils for Beechey's full-length portrait of Nelson now in St. Andrew's Hall, Norwich. This working study remained in the artist's family until 1966.

On loan to the National Portrait Gallery by the Trustees of Mr. Hugh Leggatt's Settlement.

Plate 6. Commencement of the battle of Trafalgar, October 21, 1805, by Nicholas Pocock. The *Royal Sovereign* (Vice-Admiral Collingwood) leading the starboard line in action. Pocock, a maritime artist, had in his youth commanded a trading vessel. He painted two pictures of the battle.

By permission of the National Maritime Museum.

Plate 7. The Death of Nelson by Arthur Devis. Devis went out to meet the *Victory* on her homeward passage after Trafalgar, and stayed three weeks on board, making sketches from life and on the spot.

By permission of the National Maritime Board.